The Outstanding Truth

The Outstanding Truth

Published by Charles B. M. Douglas Publishing, LLC
58 Jerusalem Road
Cohasset, MA 02025
1-781-383-0672
www.outstandingtruth.com

Cover design by White Studios
Interior design by Jomel Pepito
Publishing Consultant: Susan Hicks

Published in the United States of America
Second Edition

ISBN: 978-0-692-91826-5
1. Business & Economics / General
2. Business & Economics / Management

17.09.25

Dedication

This book is dedicated to my wife, Martha Douglas, for the patience and support she has shown during all the seemingly endless hours spent in researching and writing it.

Acknowledgments

I want to express my appreciation for the tremendous amount of time and counsel I got from Kathryn B. Earle of Touchstone Advisors of Cohasset, without whose help in editing, formatting, and recommendations it would have been far less readable.

Others who made significant observations and helpful comments include Richard P. Chapman, Jr., Paul A. Perrault, William E. Kelley, Joseph D. Steinfield, Galt Grant, Benjamin H. Lacy, Bernard A. O'Brien, George A. Barunas, Richard H. Willis, Timothy G. Greene, and other former Bank of New England employees.

In conjunction with the liquidation of the Bank of New England in 1991, the name "Bank of New England" was sold to a private party in the state of New Hampshire. That party is now operating a privately held and locally owned bank using the name "Bank of New England". No references in this book relate to that institution in any way.

Contents

Illustrations

Decker, Richard, New Yorker Cartoon 3/5/1932,
© Richard Decker/The New Yorker Collection/
www.cartoonbank.com, media ID 42266

Armstrong, Robb, New Yorker Cartoon 11/11/1996,
© Robb Armstrong/The New Yorker Collection/
www.cartoonbank.com, media ID 33225

Lorenz, Lee, New Yorker Cartoon 8/9/1976,
© Lee Lorenz/The New Yorker Collection/
www.cartoonbank.com, media ID 39614

Barsotti, Charles, New Yorker Cartoon 10/15/2007,
© Charles Barsotti/The New Yorker Collection/
www.cartoonbank.com, media ID 124431

Baldwin, Michael, Boston Globe cartoon 11/20/2007,
© Michael Baldwin/CartoonStock.com,
catalogue number mban2406

Gregory, Alex, New Yorker Cartoon 3/12/2007,
© Alex Gregory/www.cartoonbank.com, media ID
123733

Preface

Why You Should Read This Case Study

Bill Gates is quoted as having said, "It's fine to celebrate success, but it is more important to heed the lessons of failure." It seems incredible that 502 banks have failed since October 1, 2000, 320 of them in the past three and half years. This is data published by the FDIC. We clearly have not learned the lessons of failure. Thomas M. Hoenig, president of the Federal Reserve Bank of Kansas City, in his presentation[1] at the Western States Bank Directors' Education Foundation on October 30, 2006, expresses it more pointedly:

> Today, I am told that while there may be some similarities with current banking conditions and those of a quarter century ago, things are different this time. You may be hearing the same thing from investors and bankers, and, in fact you may be saying to yourself: This time, it's different. Or is it?

> Although the world has changed during the last quarter of a century, at least one thing has not—human nature. As I mentioned earlier, greed, pride, arrogance and other human frailties are often at the root of bad banking decisions, and those qualities remain with us today. They still motivate behavior as they have in the past, and, in many cases, these frailties keep us from acting on the lessons we should have learned from previous generations. In addition, no matter how sophisticated we think current analytical tools, management information systems and financial instruments are the most critical element in banking is still individual experience and judgment. In the end, bank employees, and, I would stress to this audience, bank directors, are still making the important decisions. The quality of those decisions will always depend on human characteristics and our ability to learn from the past.

The world is changing into a world economy instead of a series of local ones. For example, the distinct European currencies have been replaced by the euro, and while there were good, sound reasons for doing so, the financial impact of economic fluctuations can spread from country to country far more easily than it could when the various countries had their own distinct currencies. The switch to the euro also has resulted in exporting unsound fiscal practices, spreading more easily from country to country. We're seeing this now in destabilization in countries including Greece, Portugal, Italy, and Spain. Some European banks were adversely affected by investing in US securities backed by "securitized" subprime real estate mortgages. When that market collapsed in the United States, some of the havoc the collapse created in the United States was spread abroad. Yet it's clear that we haven't learned the lessons because years later, we're still looking for financial derivatives of one kind or another to enhance the "bottom line." In many cases, derivatives are being developed by very intelligent individuals who, nonetheless, may not have a real understanding of the risks yet whose ideas are adopted based upon their academic achievement. The people making the decisions often are convinced of the safety of the transactions by the designers, but the safeguards are not explained in a manner that is thoroughly and completely understood by those making the final decisions. As mentioned in Mr. Hoenig's presentation above, bank managers and directors are still responsible for making important decisions. The quality of those decisions will always depend on human characteristics and our ability to learn from the past. How much tragedy must there be before we make a point of learning the lessons? When will we realize it *can* happen here, then choose to prevent it?

Losses Suffered as a Result of the BNEC Bankruptcy

Bankruptcy in the United States takes essentially two forms for businesses. The first is a petition filed under Chapter 7 of the Bankruptcy Code requesting the court oversee the orderly liquidation of the business enterprise. A petition filed under Chapter 11 of the Bankruptcy

Code seeks to have the enterprise reorganized while under the protection of the court and was designed to give the debtor an opportunity to reorganize and restructure without undue pressure or harassment from creditors. In a successful reorganization, the ownership of the enterprise remains intact. Either one can be filed voluntarily by action of the board of directors or can be filed involuntarily by unsecured creditors. In each case, the court has the responsibility to see that none of the creditors is treated inequitably vis-à-vis others in the same class.

Bank of New England Corporation was petitioned into Chapter 7 of the Bankruptcy Code by the regulators and liquidated. The bank had paid dividends for 159 consecutive years until the year before its bankruptcy. With $32 billion in assets as of December 31, 1989, it was the largest commercial bank failure in New England commercial banking history and, ranked by deposit size, was one of the largest commercial bank failures in American commercial banking history: 69.4 million shares of outstanding common stock (which traded at a high of $39.125 per share in 1986 for a market value of $2,715,275,000) were rendered worthless—the stockholders were completely wiped out, the unsecured note holders were severely impaired, and retirees lost not only their savings invested in the bank's stock but also whatever value they had in unexercised options and all but $2,000 of their group life insurance coverage, life insurance that for many had represented a significant portion of their estates. The acceptable assets and deposit liabilities of the banks owned by the corporation were assumed by Fleet Bank, the unacceptable loans remained with the FDIC and were liquidated, and the balance of the corporate assets, including causes of action against third parties, were managed through liquidation by the trustee in bankruptcy. As is commented on in the staff report it also cost the federal government approximately $2.5 billion. The total loss incurred by the stockholders, note holders, and the federal government totaled some $5.7 billion in addition to the loss of group life insurance coverage in excess of $2,000 for all retirees.

Regulators' reports look into and assess the severity of problems from the outside; this book evaluates the major management deficiencies from an inside perspective. It does not attempt to address problems other than those of credit administration, although proper administration was lacking in other areas as well.

Introduction

A Disastrous Evolution

As will be pointed out in some detail in the pages that follow, the management philosophy and the assignment of responsibility at Bank of New England went through an evolution during the last forty years of its 160-year existence, the evolution accelerating during its last ten years. It began with a series of mergers and acquisitions and a change in organizational structure to accommodate the formation of lending groups to concentrate in specialized types of lending, which the bank was willing to undertake. The theory behind it was that concentration in specific market areas would enhance the bank's recognition in those sectors, enabling it to become a real factor in the markets it served. It is possible that the theory was sound, but the execution was performed in a manner that ultimately proved disastrous.

The Management Factor

Organizations have within them the seeds of their own destruction. With very few exceptions, a company's failure is the result of a deficiency in management. Strength and growth are inevitably tied into quality processes, products, and services. Solid companies have strong management, healthy product acceptance, and a reputation for quality service. They have strong financial characteristics; they can improve on existing product lines to keep abreast of changes in technology and develop new products to enter new markets or have the muscle to enter markets established by others.

While it is true that some companies may transition from strong to weak in a surprisingly short time due to changes in management philosophy, generally the management of large well-respected companies tends to change incrementally over time, with the result that the effects of those changes, positive and negative, may not be outwardly apparent for some time, in some cases several years. In addition, a company's reputation for traditional high quality can sometimes obscure the effects of gradual adverse changes from investors, regulators (in the case of banks), accountants, and in some cases, from the board of directors until their cumulative effect becomes overwhelming. The Bank of New England provides a strong illustration of this.

Drawing organization charts and filling in the boxes with functions, names, and titles is a useless exercise if management deigns to reign but not rule. There is no room for complacency in management. A paternalistic management tends to fill the boxes in the organization charts with the names of those who are favored and with those with whom they feel comfortable, regardless of any demonstrated ability to perform the job, and feel that all the bases are covered. Businesses are run by people, and their ability to perform all of the required tasks in an intelligent, coordinated manner will determine the degree to which the business succeeds or fails. As for the competent manager, essential qualities include the ability to select and train subordinates well, delegate responsibility and authority to those who are qualified to discharge those duties, and remove those who are not; otherwise, the organization will ultimately founder. As mentioned above, established companies may be managed well for many years, only to be destroyed from within due to cronyism and complacency in senior management. At the Bank of New England, National Association (BNENA), for at least ten years, the managerial positions were often filled by people who did not necessarily understand their new responsibilities. This problem was compounded by the presumption of competence. In spite of warning signs to the contrary and operating deficiencies clearly pointed out in Loan Review reports and other internal memos, the increasing risks went unchecked.

Some companies founded and run by people with *no* formal college degree have been extremely successful; William Gates of Microsoft and Thomas Edison are cases in point. Obviously, the lack of an MBA does not necessarily translate into a deficiency in management skills. A master's degree in business administration, on the other hand, does not automatically ensure the ability to be an effective administrator. It is not unusual for an individual to excel academically but to lack the personality traits necessary for effective leadership. Bank of New England had some charismatic managers who may well have been good academic students, but who were incompetent managers with poor leadership skills, including indecisiveness, an inability to exert discipline when called for, and inability to get things done in a timely manner. It is symptomatic of a style of management that promotes on the basis of personal relationships rather than on an objective assessment of ability. It may appear to succeed for a while, but it inherently nourishes those seeds of its own destruction. It is only human nature for subordinates to emulate the management styles of their superiors, and once a paternalistic pattern has been established, it ultimately permeates the entire organization and is very difficult to break. At BNENA, refusal on the part of senior management to recognize and act on such deficiencies in their peers and subordinates when poor results were evident exacerbated the problems inherent in a flawed system, which separated responsibility from authority and, in so doing, sacrificed accountability.

The Strength of Knowing When to Ask for Help

Capable management is conscious of its own limitations and controls its growth accordingly or acquires new and capable talent as needed; corporate size alone is not necessarily an indicator of good management. A good example of a small company management's recognition of its own limitations and effective remedial action would be the case of a small company founded in the 1960s by an engineer to develop and produce microwave components. Sales grew; the company expanded its workforce and was profitable until the third year when, for the first time, sales exceeded $1,000,000. That year the company lost money. After a careful analysis, the owner determined that the loss was attributable to his inability to control all of the necessary functions himself and his inability to delegate effectively to others. He pulled back on his bidding for jobs to the point where he could personally oversee the production requirements of the contracts the company took and handle the administrative requirements of the business as well. His volume dropped below the $1,000,000 level, and he returned to profitability. In the case of the microwave component manufacturer, it was largely coincidence that the million-dollar sales level coincided with his upper breakeven point, but dollar volumes of businesses are often benchmarks of administrative capacity. Larger revenues translate into the requirement for a new business model, often entailing more employees, more supervisors, and more control mechanisms. Each phase requires effective delegation of responsibility and authority because with each phase of growth, senior management becomes more removed from the details, and reliance on the competence of subordinates increases.

There is any amount of material that purports to help develop the skills to run a company effectively, but little to help managers promoted beyond their capacity to recognize and face their own shortcomings, let alone admit them to their superiors. It also takes courage for managers to recognize the shortcomings in subordinates they have promoted and to take effective action, either to replace them with qualified personnel or to develop them (if the new responsibilities are limited). Performance failure is a topic people prefer not to face honestly when it involves the possibility of their own poor judgment; it is quite common to attribute the consequences of their own behavior to the failure of others to perform adequately or to the lack of understanding of extraneous elements, such as "unreasonable" bank examiners whom they regard as being unduly harsh in their criticisms of the loan portfolio and the manner in which it is being managed. Consistent sound management philosophy generally requires that tenures in positions of senior management be of some duration. Frequent management changes are a clear warning sign of unsettled and ineffective management. Bank of New England made frequent changes in the Credit Policy Officer, who was responsible for the administration of the loan portfolio, and other senior management positions, as chronicled in the following section.

Richard Driscoll was executive vice president and Credit Policy Officer from the late 1970s to 1985. He became chairman of the Senior Loan Approval Committee (SLAC) in 1981 and retained that position after being promoted to president in 1985. Robert McAlear, SVP in charge of Boston Community Banking, succeeded him as Credit Policy Officer for a short period in 1985, only to be promoted to EVP and put in charge of the Commercial Finance Department when the head of that department left the bank. McAlear was replaced as Credit Policy Officer by Hugh M. Taylor in 1985. Thomas Wilson, formerly head of Commercial Banking, was made president of BNENA in 1987, when Driscoll was promoted to chairman of BNENA, and Wilson assumed the chairmanship of the SLAC. In 1987, Taylor was put in charge of Commercial Banking to replace Thomas Wilson, and David Falwell, a lending group leader, was promoted to EVP and became Credit Policy Officer at that point, remaining as such through 1989.

Tacit Agreement to Present Favorably

An argument can be made that there is a distinction between financial and economic failure. Financial failure is defined as operating at a loss to the point where the company's capital position is severely impaired and continued operations may well result in bankruptcy, as was the case with Bank of New England Corporation. Economic failure could be described as inefficient use of capital, such as the profitability of the enterprise being insufficient to support the level of required capital investment. The demarcation line is a fine one for it essentially means that if invested elsewhere, the capital could earn "more." On the other hand, capital is not generally readily transferred to other endeavors, and many businesses carry on with marginal profitability or break-even operations for an extended time. In this condition, however, they are very vulnerable to changes in business conditions and present an undue risk for lending institutions. A case in point would be Pan American Airways (Pan Am). Although operating at a loss, Pan Am was able to continue operating and continued to retain its bank-revolving credit for many years based upon its positive cash flow, in this case cash flow being defined as net earnings plus depreciation. Aircraft are normally depreciated as rapidly as the taxing authorities allow while, with proper maintenance and periodic retrofits, the useful life of the equipment far exceeds the depreciation period. The heavy depreciation and marginal operating results were reflected in net losses on the income statements and concomitant reduction in equity, but the cash flow (as defined) was positive. The rationale for continued financial support was that the reported losses would become profits when the depreciation charges were eliminated. Its long-term economic viability was clearly questionable as the erosion of equity had left the airline highly leveraged, and operations were marginal at best and had been for some time. When increased competition among international airlines resulted in lower fares, Pan Am was no longer able to compete and was among the first to fail. A somewhat similar attempt to see results of operations in a more favorable light than submitted financial statements reflected occurred at BNE. As a result of pressure brought to bear on the Credit Administration Division by one of the lending groups, the Credit Department was instructed to spread financial statements presented by some types of borrowers on a FIFO accounting basis rather than the LIFO basis on which they were submitted when the LIFO presentation indicated losses or marginal operating results. (See chapter entitled "Credit Administration Policies.") In other words, the Credit Administration Division tacitly agreed with the account officers to modify the submitted financial statements to reflect operating results, which would justify the extension of credit.

Failure to Meet Basic Fiduciary Responsibility

It is not unusual for the aggressive management style of some companies engaged in competitive industries (banking being among them) to reach for a rate of growth greater than that of their peers and, in the process, allow sound judgment to be eroded for the sake of volume. The introduction to the staff report to the Committee on Banking, Finance, and Urban Affairs of the US House of Representatives in December 1991 follows:

US House of Representatives
Committee on Banking, Finance and Urban Affairs

One Hundred Second Congress
2129 Rayburn House Office Building
Washington, DC 20515

To: Members of the Committee on Banking, Finance and Urban Affairs

Transmitted with this letter is a staff report on the costly failure of the Bank of New England.

The Bank was declared insolvent on January 6, 1991 and is one of the 1,000 federally insured banks that failed in the past five years.

The study provides the most thorough autopsy of a major bank collapse ever undertaken by the Committee. The study was ordered after this Committee uncovered major deficiencies in the operation and regulation of the Bank during hearings on January 9, 1991 and June 13, 1991.

The study reveals a management strategy based on a high-risk gamble on commercial real estate without proper internal controls. The money on the gambling table, of course, was publically [sic] insured money—at least $2.5 billion of which will never be recovered. Management and the board of directors failed to meet their basic fiduciary responsibility to operate the Bank of New England in a safe and sound manner.

In theory, we have a regulatory system that steps in and requires corrective action when management fails to meet its responsibility. But, this "fail-safe" regulatory system failed at the Bank of New England as miserably as did management in ensuring that the Bank operated in a safe and sound manner and protected insured deposits.

As the study points out, the problems at the Bank of New England are not new to the banking industry. In 1984, the Continental Illinois Bank in Chicago failed and the same lack of internal controls and the same urge to play long-shot gambles were evident when the dry rot of that institution was pulled apart. And surprise—many of the hand-wringing, timid and inadequate regulatory responses were present in that mammoth 1984 failure. Clearly, Federal regulators learn slowly from their mistakes.

In the Bank of New England case, the examiners at the Office of the Comptroller of the Currency spotted serious problems as early as 1987, but it was not until 1990 that OCC could bring itself to initiate definitive action. By then, it was too late and it became a question of just how big the losses would be for the Bank Insurance Fund. OCC could have acted sooner. It could have been much more forceful in demanding changes at the Bank.

The Congress has just refinanced the Bank Insurance Fund through a $30 billion line of credit at the US Treasury. Even with the recapitalization, the strains on the fund are extremely heavy and, unfortunately, the next line of defense is a bailout of the industry financed by the taxpayers. We cannot afford another Bank of New England. Most particularly, we cannot afford a "too little, too late" regulatory system.

In the Federal Deposit Insurance Corporation Improvement Act of 1991 passed by the Congress on November 27 of this year, extensive new powers are given to the regulators. The

> additional authority is designed to create a regulatory force that can spot problems early and take definitive action before banks become basket cases and huge liabilities for the insurance fund.
>
> However, Congress has adopted many supervisory reforms in the past only to see regulators ignore, dodge or mismanage the statutory instructions. This time, Congress must keep a close watch on how these new regulatory authorities are implemented in the different agencies. I intend to ask the General Accounting Office to assemble a special task force to monitor the implementation of the new laws and report to the Congress at regular and frequent intervals on these supervisory issues. In adopting the new statute, the Congress has instructed the regulators to take "prompt action" when deficiencies are identified. I want Congress to be in the same position to take prompt action if regulation continues to fail and if new statutory improvements are needed.
>
> This study of the Bank of New England collapse provides extremely valuable case history of management and regulatory failure. Bank of New England must be a lesson learned, not repeated.
>
> Henry B. Gonzales
> Chairman

As in Thomas Hoenig's comments quoted in the prologue, Gonzalez refers here to the apparent inability of bank officers, directors, and regulators to learn from mistakes of the past, although the comments were made some sixteen years apart. In the case of Bank of New England, there was not only the argument that "this time it's different," but also the blind and euphoric belief that "that could never happen here!" because all of the boxes in the organization charts were filled, the demand for commercial real estate loans was rising, and Loan Operations (the division responsible for the data-processing needs of the bank) was generating a multitude of reports. Nobody took the time to try to find out exactly what did happen "there." Had they done so, they would have recognized that there were some alarming similarities between the manner in which Continental Bank in Chicago had grown and failed and the rapid growth of BNENA. In both cases, internal controls were weakened to the point of ineffectiveness by subordination to marketing efforts and by other deep-seated leadership problems that effectively separated responsibility from authority and, by so doing, created an atmosphere of confusion in which *nobody* felt accountable. The remainder of this case study is presented in the following chapters in the hope that you and fellow leaders, managers, and students in the financial and business world today will keep in mind the pitfalls described and avoid them. If you learn from these lessons of the past and apply that knowledge, it will provide a firm basis for sustained growth and profitability.

Bank of New England: An Evolution in Management (1950–1991)

The First Acquisitions

The first acquisition during this period was the Pilgrim Trust Company acquired in the mid-1950s. Pilgrim was a small Boston bank that catered to clients of a slightly lower credit standard than the traditional Merchants National Bank customers. Its loans and lending staff continued to be housed in the old Pilgrim quarters although the name disappeared, and from an organizational standpoint, its staff was added to the staff of Merchants National Bank and the loan portfolios were consolidated. Shortly thereafter, the bank merged with the New England Trust Company. The loan portfolio was merged with that of the Merchants National Bank, and its lending and senior executive staffs were consolidated and moved into the Merchants National Bank head office. Trust Department functions were moved to the old New England Trust Company building. The name was changed to New England Merchants National Bank. The bank subsequently formed a holding company through which various small banks throughout eastern Massachusetts were acquired, each maintaining its individual staff and loan portfolio. With the pending acquisition of the Conifer Group of banks and a merger with the Connecticut Bank and Trust Company in the mid-1980s, the name of the holding company was changed to Bank of New England Corp., and the New England Merchants National Bank became Bank of New England, National Association, referred to in this book and in various exhibits as Bank of New England or simply as BNE or BNENA. Connecticut Bank and Trust Company is often referred to as CBT.

A History of Conservatism

In the early 1950s, the banking side of Merchants National Bank (as opposed to the "trust" side) was strictly what is known as a wholesale bank (i.e., one dealing almost exclusively in business loans and services rather than in consumer services). It had two offices, one at 28 State Street and one at Copley Square in the New England Life Building in Boston. Richard P. Chapman had recently been named the president and chairman, and he had been with the bank, primarily in the Trust Department, since his graduation from Harvard Business School in the mid-1920s. In his mid-forties, he was fairly young in comparison to the rest of the official staff. Mr. Chapman sat in a small corner office; the lending vice presidents sat on what was known as the platform at the rear of the narrow marble-lined banking lobby, with its high ceilings and its black metal grillwork separating the tellers' cages that stretched down one side almost to the front door from the rest of the lobby. Each officer sat behind a wooden rolltop desk with a heavy brass nameplate placed on top. The atmosphere was conservative and accurately reflected the attitude of the bank's management.

The bank training program differed from those of other Boston banks in some respects. Trainees at other Boston banks typically became officers within two to three years but were given limited lending authority at that point. At Merchants it took five to six years, during which one spent time in each of the operating departments and then went to the Credit Department for training as a lending officer. Once you became a lending officer at the Merchants, however, you were authorized to lend amounts up to the bank's legal limit on your own signature without the need for senior approval. As a practical matter, loan requests generally came to the senior officers, and they would turn them over to the junior officers assigned to them; very few lending decisions were made without some consultation. Because of the conservative culture and lengthy training lending officers received, losses overall were exceptionally low. In the early 1960s, the bank capitalized on the authority given its officers in its advertising campaigns featuring the "Where the man you talk to is the bank" line that ran successfully for many years. At one point, the bank's ads even claimed, "It takes two to say 'No.'"

Compromise of Individual Responsibility

During the 1960s the training changed, the time spent in operating departments was all but eliminated, and the required years of credit analysis, credit investigations, and apprenticeship were materially shortened. Perhaps the broad authority became inappropriate in the late 1960s and early 1970s as a consequence. In any event, during the 1970s restrictive individual lending authorities were assigned and loan approval committees were established. The "man you talk to" was no longer the bank. While some type of transition was called for, somewhere in the process individual accountability became compromised. A formal senior loan approval committee was established, chaired by the senior lending officer, and all loans above $1,000,000 were presented to the committee. Here the real obfuscation of responsibility or accountability began to set in for the committee regarded itself as a sounding board, not an approval board, and the responsibility for the loans it "approved" remained, presumably, with the individual lending officers who had presented them. At this point, it became difficult from a practical standpoint to tell where delegation of authority ended and abdication of responsibility began. The eroding effects on discipline in loan management by both groups and individuals went unaddressed.

Development of Specialty Lending Groups

As the size of the bank's loan portfolio grew, there was a gradual development of specialty commercial lending groups designed to handle specific types of loans. The first step was the establishment of the Consumer Credit Department in the early 1950s. It was staffed largely by personnel hired from well-regarded consumer finance companies. Personal installment loans were the first step; the effort soon expanded into automobile financing and, to enhance the flow of business, spread into automobile floor plan financing for automobile dealers. The official staff of the Consumer Credit Department clearly had not had the same degree of training in traditional commercial lending as the "graduates" of the bank training program, and the senior management of the bank had little or no experience in consumer finance. While nominally responsible to a vice president in the commercial lending area, as a practical matter the responsibility for generating and approving all of the loans in the department was left to the personnel of the Consumer Credit Department. The consumer portfolio experienced average performance for the nature of the portfolio. The floor plan loans were really more akin to commercial loans for inventory financing, however, and given the singular lack of commercial loan training, the portfolio suffered substantial losses. The bank ultimately got out of the floor plan financing business altogether. The responsibility and the accountability for the losses was somewhat defused between the "nobody told me not to" feeling on the part of the department management on the one hand, and the "we knew they had no commercial lending experience and we should have recognized the floor plan loans for the commercial loans they were" on the part of the bank senior management on the other.

Growth of Commercial Lending

The next step was the establishment of the Commercial Finance Department in 1960. Although it was a departure from the traditionally high-quality lending on which the Bank had been built, banks had been lending to commercial finance companies for years, and while certainly more marginal than the rest of the commercial loan portfolio, it was, nonetheless, lending to commercial businesses where many of the same analytical concepts applied. The department was established to specialize in making loans of a more marginal nature, secured by the assignment of accounts receivable and inventories. The first loans transferred into the department were those from other parts of the loan portfolio, which seemed, for the most part, to have some of the characteristics of loans typically made by commercial finance companies. Also added were those loans that had been made to finance production under government contracts because they were secured, in part, by filing a security interest in the company's accounts receivable under the contracts and inventories acquired to fulfill them. The security interest was "perfected" by filing under the Assignment of Claims Act of 1940 (an act passed in 1940 to encourage commercial banks to lend to companies handling production under government contracts by granting them a first security interest that was free of offsets in contracts being financed) as well as the required filings with the city and state. The official staff of the department had had the traditional credit training and, because of the collateral management capabilities, was soon delegated the responsibility for handling the workout loans for which responsibility for lending decisions rested with the "Controlled Loan Committee." The Commercial Finance Department (CFD) reported to the senior lending officer of the bank, and new proposals were presented on a weekly basis for informational purposes to a commercial lending committee consisting of the senior lending staff of the bank. In theory, each of the lending officers had the authority to lend up to the bank's legal limit, but as a practical matter, all loans of any consequence were discussed at the weekly commercial lending committee meeting. While the procedure was designed to be protective of loan quality, it had the side effect of diluting responsibility to some degree as, unless there was an outspoken objection to a loan being discussed, it was assumed that tacit agreement had been reached.

There was little competition among banks for the commercial finance type of financing (i.e., lending to small companies secured by the assignment of their accounts receivable and inventories). The Uniform Commercial Code (UCC) was adopted by the various states in the early 1960s to provide established procedures for obtaining a valid security interest in a borrower's assets. After its adoption, banks could obtain a security interest in the borrower's assets without having to monitor the asset levels in detail. They began to lend to small businesses secured by a blanket lien on all of the borrower's assets without having to exercise jurisdiction over the assets, as previously required to perfect a security interest. This differed from what was called commercial finance lending, which followed the same procedures applied by the commercial finance companies where assets pledged as collateral were closely monitored and funds received by the borrower's account debtors were remitted to the lender and applied to the loans. Bank of New England operated its Commercial Finance Department in much the same fashion as the commercial finance companies, including the periodic assignment of new accounts receivable generated by the borrower, remittance by borrowers of all funds received in payment of accounts receivable, application of remittances to outstanding loan balances, and periodic examination of the borrowers' books and records. As indicated above, its portfolio originally consisted of loans transferred into it from various areas of the bank, many of them being loans to companies performing under prime government contracts and secured by appropriate filings under the Assignment of Claims Act of 1940. It soon branched out into other types of businesses to include a cross section of wholesalers and manufacturers doing business in the New England states. While the Bank of Boston had had a factoring operation for some time, Bank of New England became the first to specialize in commercial finance lending and grew rapidly. Its growth came from the fact that its lending rates were substantially lower than commercial finance company rates (on the order of 8% versus finance company rates of 18%), and the risks it was willing to assume were only slightly better. When a borrower showed signs of weakness, however, the borrower was forced to refinance with another lender, generally a commercial finance company, as the bank had consciously made the decision not to become a lender of last resort. Its growth prompted complaints from some of the finance companies to which the bank extended lines of credit that the bank was putting them out of business in the acceptable loan markets and was forcing them into the marginal-loan markets. The Commercial Finance Department became one of the largest commercial finance operations in the northeast.

Many specialty groups, when they have experienced a certain amount of success in one area, tend to feel that they can use the same financing technique in other areas where the basics are really quite different. Commercial finance was no exception. The formula of the lending approach (i.e., advancing a percentage of the value of accounts receivable and finished goods inventory) was successful because the collateral generally had reliable value—receivables were due from third parties for goods delivered, and raw materials or finished goods could usually be sold for fifty cents on the dollar. The success led to expansion into lending the same percentages against the accounts receivable and inventories of other types of business, specifically technology firms where the receivables were often progress payments due under contracts. Since they were not always prime contractors, the Assignment of Claims Act of 1940 was not available to provide protection against offsets if a contract were not completed, so the value of these receivables as collateral would be seriously impaired if one were forced to rely on them, and since the inventory consisted primarily of work in process, it was virtually worthless in liquidation. The lessons learned were expensive, and for a time, the bank confined its commercial finance lending to a more traditional practice. As is commented on elsewhere in the section of "Misapplied Principles," the lessons eventually were forgotten.

As time went on, other new lending specialty areas were developed to capitalize on the potential for loan growth offered in specific markets. Eventually, the specialty groups would come to include real estate, national accounts, energy, high tech, and communications in addition to commercial finance and consumer lending. Loan operations were originally split into groups reporting to different section heads, later reporting to Credit Administration for loans generated by BNENA. Loan operations functions were subsequently consolidated into a central corporate operations group in the mid-1980s to late 1980s.

Clashing Cultures and Risky Role Transitions

In retrospect, the nature of traditional bank lending efforts had evolved from one of responding to requests for loans to one of seeking lending opportunities; with that evolution came an increasing consideration for the business-generating potential of people being hired into the lending function. While still strong, the emphasis on strong credit skills had begun to erode; hiring officers from other banks for their perceived business generating skills, once frowned on, gradually became an accepted practice; new officer positions were established for selling cash management and processing services; and increasing emphasis was placed on generating fee income. Although it was not necessarily perceived as such at the time, Boston banking was entering a lengthy period of clashing cultures, intensified competition, and a groping struggle for a clearer role for banks in the broad area encompassing all financial services. The struggle was, and still is, characterized by frequent excesses in lending activities and development of new "products" or services in areas with an alarming array of unknowns. Virtually none of the ramifications for the industry have been considered; many staffing, administration, integration, marketing, competitive and management requirements have not been thought through; the markets are not completely understood; and the risks have not been properly researched. Somewhere in the evolution process at Bank of New England, common sense was sacrificed for the appearance of diversified corporate growth. Below are three brief excerpts from the Bank of New England 10-K[2] issued in the spring of 1990 and covering the year 1989.

> As previously announced, the Corporation has consented to a cease and desist order with the Fed, dated February 26, 1990, and Bank of New England, N.A. ("BNE, NA") has consented to

a cease and desist order issued by the OCC, dated February 26, 1990 (together, the "consent orders"). The consent orders are filed as exhibits to the Corporation's Current Report on Form 8-1 filed with the Securities and Exchange Commission dated as of February 26, 1990. The following description of the consent orders is qualified in its entirety by reference to the full text of the consent order. The Connecticut Bank and Trust Company, NA, Bank of New England-West, NA, Bank of New England-Old Colony, NA, and Maine National Bank are expected to sign similar consent orders within the next month.

The consent orders deal comprehensively with the development and implementation of plans, policies, and procedures to improve the operations and condition of the Corporation and its subsidiary banks, particularly in the areas of asset quality, management, loan administration, and capital. The consent orders address a broad range of deficiencies in the operations and conditions of the Corporation and its subsidiary banks identified by the regulators. In accordance with the consent orders, the Corporation is in the process of finalizing capital, strategy, and debt service plans to submit to the regulators for review and approval.

... The response to the Corporation's capital and liquidity problems has been a decision to downsize the Corporation by approximately

> one-third. Approximately $8 billion of specific loan and investment assets have been liquidated or are being marketed for sale. Sales and other dispositions of approximately $4 billion in assets will generate approximately $175 million of gains in the first quarter of 1990.
>
> ... The Corporation's strategic plan will include an effort to significantly reduce operating costs while concentrating on its primary franchise businesses of consumer banking, trust and private banking, and middle-market commercial lending. Certain lines of business which do not fit into these primary franchise businesses are being downsized or eliminated. They include processing services, large corporate banking outside of New England, leasing, discount brokerage, and other low-margin, high-labor or high-technology businesses. Although some of these lines have contributed to earnings in the past, their elimination will help to downsize the balance sheet and to concentrate management's attention on the areas of greatest strength and potential. The Corporation expects to recognize certain significant one-time costs, including severance costs, in connection with its expense reduction programs which are being reviewed.

The "strategic plan" referred to was an attempt to comply with the requirement of the federal regulatory agencies that the bank increase its liquidity and eliminate loans they classified as being heavily leveraged transactions and loans to companies in certain lines of business altogether.

Mismanagement and Mortality

At one of its regular weekly meetings in the late 1980s, the Senior Loan Approval Committee (SLAC) met to discuss a several million dollar leasing proposal for Xerox, and all of the members were there, including the head of the bank's international division, who generally skipped the meetings because, as he said, "I don't really know much about commercial credit." He attended this meeting, however, because he was interested in the reaction the rest of the members would have to the Xerox proposal. When it came up on the agenda for discussion, he commented that he thought the company should be rated a 6 (Special Mention [i.e., below generally acceptable loan standards]) because the company was dying in spite of the results shown on the balance sheet and operating statements. Basically, he felt that it had not kept pace and that the rest of the industry was too far ahead for them to catch up. He ultimately turned out to be wrong. As he looked at the Xerox data prepared for the committee, the chairman of the Senior Loan Approval Committee commented that he wasn't sure the concept that companies are immortal was correct and that all companies probably had a finite life span. I was reminded of an occasion some twenty years earlier. Richard P. Chapman was then chairman of the board and president of the bank. I had been called into his office to discuss a threatened lawsuit. I told him that the case had no legal merit, and he asked, "Are we morally obligated?" When I replied we were not, he said, "Then let him sue 'til hell freezes over. You and I are mortal, but this bank is not, and as a corporation, it will go on forever." Unfortunately, the chairman of the Senior Loan Approval Committee was right, and Mr. Chapman's comment about the bank's being immortal was not. He had overlooked the fact that the success of an institution is not necessarily a permanent state; prosperity and failure are results of management behavior, and management philosophy and ability can and do change over time. The ultimate failure of the bank was due to management deficiency—ineffective leadership due to weakness of character and lack of leadership capability that, in turn, led to misguided acquisitions, to promotion of individuals for personal reasons rather than proven ability and qualification for the job, and to erosion of loan standards for the sake of competitive growth. It had taken over 145 years to build the bank into one of the finest regional banks in the country, and it took another fifteen years of increasing emphasis on unbridled growth and erosion of sound management principles to destroy it.

"Fundamentally, the ship was sound."

Applying the Lessons from the Past

Balancing Growth with Risk

It would be unusual for the volume of financial restructurings not to decline dramatically as the economic conditions in which the borrowers and lenders operate improve, and such has been the case. Attention to financial restructurings will increase when the excesses resulting from competition begin to reappear. During the lean years, companies trimmed excess personnel, controlled their inventories, and improved efficiency. In the years that followed, they enjoyed a predictable resurgence in sales without a need for increased borrowing, financial institutions being liquid following several years of reduced demand for borrowed funds. As a result, the marked concern that financial institutions once had for the quality of their loan portfolios shifted to the challenges of growth and improved "operating ratios." Attention in commercial banks focused on loan portfolio growth, cost reduction, maximization of fee income, and the market price of their stock. Attention should also have been focused on maintaining the organizational balance needed to assure that the appropriate checks and balances were in place to monitor risk exposure in all activities as well as in portfolio quality and adherence to policy. Subordinating basic bank management and bank lending principles, when competition in traditional markets becomes heated and emphasis on stock performance, becomes an overriding concern. Credit standards are often lowered for the sake of volume—a disastrous strategy.

Commercial banks exist in very competitive markets and operate on narrow spreads over the total cost of funds. On the whole, their capacity for risk is limited by their relatively highly leveraged financial condition. On the other hand, they are judged by the investment community and by their peers on the return on assets and equity, growth rate, and comparative "efficiency" (the ratio of noninterest expense to total revenue). The soundness of their portfolios and business practices tends to be taken for granted, and the relatively limited ability to absorb losses is often overlooked. Because of the emphasis placed on operating statistics, the pressure to perform well in the marketplace results in efforts to (a) increase interest income through both increased loan volume and maintenance of interest rate spreads, (b) reduce noninterest expense, and (c) increase fee income from common and novel finance-related transactions such as standby letters of credit, foreign exchange trading, and dealing in financial derivatives.

The paradox is that in the process of innovating, improving efficiency, and streamlining their reporting structures, controls often are unwittingly weakened, and economies of scale are obtained at the expense of proper portfolio management.

1. In order to increase the balance of loans outstanding while maintaining current spreads, banks may begin to compete on the basis of more flexible underwriting standards rather than on interest rates charged.

2. Account officers may be expected to generate more loans and to handle increased numbers of accounts without regard for proper account and file maintenance.

3. Budgets for functions not engaged in income-generating activity, such as credit administration or internal audit, may restrict the hiring of needed personnel, resulting in a reduction in the ability to monitor portfolio quality and compliance with policy properly.

4. Banks may become more actively engaged in dealing in financial products or transactions for which neither all of the risk ramifications nor the necessary checks and balances are fully understood within the institution.

The sine qua non for extension of credit is the ability of the borrower to repay its debts and the ability of the analyst to determine the financial capability of the borrower to repay. Collateral is never a good substitute for repayment capacity. Collateral should be regarded only as a *secondary* source of repayment to be used in the *unlikely* event of borrower failure. Unfortunately, the desire of department heads for the management recognition that comes with growing loan volume and the pressure by management to increase market share result in erosion of this principle; many lenders gradually come to rely *primarily* on collateral rather than on demonstrated financial capability. To make a bad practice worse, the methodology of collateral evaluation, particularly in the case of innovative financing, relies heavily on the judgment of the account officer and on hearsay evidence from associates rather than on hard facts or past experience. Good examples of the widespread acceptance of this kind of thinking and its consequences are the overreliance on oil prices during the 1970s and early 1980s and real estate prices in the mid-1980s to late 1980s that, when prices fell to more normal levels, forced many banking institutions into liquidation. The lenders succumbed to the pressures of the market and based upon the assumption that the values of oil and of real estate would continue to rise, they leaned far too heavily on collateral rather than on the financial stability of the borrowers. When oil and real estate prices fell instead of rising, over-leveraged borrowers went under, and very substantial losses were suffered by the lenders. Bank of New England went under as a result of overly aggressive lending in real estate and communications, but the reasoning was there in virtually all areas where asset-based lending was conducted. Instead of basing the loans on careful credit analyses, the practice simply became one of lending (i.e., making loans secured by the assignment of assets as collateral) with advances based on a percentage of the assumed value rather than on demonstrated ability to repay. This was particularly the case with the loans generated by the Customer Service Offices (offices established in other states in which state laws did not allow banks from other states to operate as banks but allowed them to generate leads, which would then be followed up and the loans made by the home office).

Lender of Last Resort

Following is an excerpt of a memo written by the SVP Loan Control on January 19, 1983, to Richard Driscoll, then Credit Policy Officer[3].

> While collateral-based lending is desirable, there is a tendency to be complacent with loans to borrowers whose financial condition is deteriorating as long as collateral coverage appears adequate, rather than moving the loan out. The result is that by the time action is taken to force the loan out, it is too late to do so and we have become the lender of last resort. Is that consciously the role we want to play? I think inherent danger is the tendency on the part of the group leader or his contact officer to rely too much on the strength of collateral represented by numbers which may, in turn, have no economic reality. Examples of this can

> be found in the files for Thor, Currier, Dovre and any one of a dozen shipping loans.

Driscoll replied to the memo by saying that he had discussed the issue of last-resort lender with the head of the Commercial Finance Department and that the department head felt comfortable with that position. The problem with that approach was that Loan Operations was not set up to track receivables collateral in the same manner that a lender of last resort on accounts receivable would normally employ (i.e., on a ledgered basis), receiving copies of all invoices from the borrower, posting them to individual account ledgers, applying payments to them as remittances came in from a lockbox account, and notifying the borrower of the specific invoices that had been paid by the account debtors. In many cases, the last-resort lender will request that all account debtors be informed of the assignment of the accounts and be requested to remit directly to the lender. The degree to which reliance on collateral can be both misleading and dangerous comes from three sources, one being the borrower who submits fraudulent collateral information in order to support the loan balance; another is the borrower who receives payment from the account debtor but retains the funds for his own use without informing the lender of the payment. The third is the account officer or district manager who feels that disclosure of the true value of collateral would result in having the loan downgraded and transferred out of his control—in the case of Bank of New England, to the Controlled Loan Department. A case in point is Dovre Ski, mentioned above.

Dovre Ski manufactured fittings and bindings for the ski industry; sales and production were very seasonal in nature, as were their customers. This resulted in an uneven financial support cycle—heavy reliance on inventory support at one point, heavy reliance on receivables at another. The company had been a customer of the bank for many years, although the management and current ownership had been in place for only a few years. In addition to accounts receivable and inventories, the bank held a lien on the real estate and on a condominium owned by one of the principals. In order to assist in the inventory financing, the company received a percentage advance against its inventory and was allowed to borrow at a receivable advance rate against inventory produced under contract for large buyers who would take delivery of the goods when their selling season opened. Inventory so produced was classified as a "bill and hold" (i.e., the company would bill their customer for the goods, but the goods would be stored at the company until delivery when the products would be shipped and paid for under the terms of the orders). After the season started and shipments began, the bulk of loan balance would be supported by receivables. In order to boost sales, the company offered a return policy to some of its smaller customers, under which material not used or sold at the end of their season could be returned and credits would be issued for the returns.

Shortly after having been reviewed at a loan review meeting at which the district group leader had indicated that the loan was sound and that the staleness of many the receivables was not an issue since the old accounts would be paid up as soon as the season started, the company filed for protection under Chapter 11 of the Bankruptcy Code. Our collateral position was grim. It was the beginning of the production season, making the prospect of liquidating an out-of-season work in process inventory most unattractive, and the receivables consisted largely of bill-and-hold accounts (advance orders from large customers for goods to be delivered as called for after their selling season had begun) and the past-due accounts from smaller account debtors that ostensibly would be paid at the beginning of the season. The court approved the hiring of a business consultant, and the Controlled Loan Department of the bank agreed to provide debtor-in-possession financing. After reviewing the collateral records, the bank examiners deemed it inadequate to support the loan level and requested a $250,000 charge-off.

The consultant had only been on the job for a short period when he called the head of Loan Control to report that the old receivables on the books were worthless as they should have been offset by issued credits months before. According to the company's management, the reason they had not issued the credits and the accounts had not been deleted on the company's books was the request from the old account officer at the bank not to write them off because doing so would render the company insolvent on the financial statements submitted to the bank, and the loan would have to be transferred to the Controlled Loan Department. The rationale was apparently that the bank was not lending anything against the past-due accounts in any event, so there was no harm in leaving them on the books. The consultant also reported that a lot of the inventory that had been made to fill bill-and-hold orders and, included in the receivable base they were borrowing against, had been sold to others rather than held for fulfillment of the contracts; yet the collateral reported to the bank did not reflect a commensurate reduction in the bill-and-hold receivables. The receivables generated by what should have been segregated inventory were in turn borrowed against. To make matters worse, a wing that had been added to the manufacturing building was located over the septic system leaching field, and a crack had developed in the floor. The result was that whenever the number of employees exceeded a certain level, the septic fluid would seep up through the floor, thus restricting the number of workers at the time when the manufacturing should have been at its peak. While we held a lien on the building, its collateral value was questionable.

The consultant was finally able to negotiate the sale of the company to another larger competitor and liquidate the rest of the collateral. Our final loss was reduced to $100,000.

Dovre raised several issues, not the least of which was the overreliance on the reported value of collateral, in this case the borrower's inflation of collateral values by inclusion of inventory in bill-and-hold accounts treated as receivables when inventory had in fact been removed and sold to others whose receivables, in turn, were borrowed against. A second issue was the failure to notify the bank that the old accounts receivable were in fact offset by unissued credits, which, had they been issued, would have eliminated the company's net worth. Another issue was the deliberate delay in the transfer of a troubled loan to the Controlled Loan Department in hopes that the situation would somehow fix itself.

Progressive Weakening of Control in the Name of Growth

Repeated attempts to address the issues raised by Loan Review and Loan Control were singularly unsuccessful, perhaps for the reasons mentioned in the chapter on credit administration. Below is an excerpt from the confidential memo dated June 23, 1983, to Richard Driscoll, then Credit Policy Officer and chairman of the Senior Loan Approval Committee, and as such, the senior lending officer of the bank[4].

> The loan portfolio of the Bank is increasing in size, complexity and geographical origin. At the same time, I feel that our control, both in terms of credit handling and credit approval, is getting relatively weaker. This is brought about not by a decrease in Loan Review or Controlled Loan capability, but rather by an increase in the lending staff where credit skills have been downplayed in favor of selling ability, by an increasing reluctance on the part of lending groups to have their loans classified anywhere

below an existing #3 rating, with resulting pressure being put on credit analysts, by a desire on the part of contact staff to "handle their own problems" where that desire is shared by the group leaders, and by a deterioration in the basic quality of credit analyses.

With the change in LAC requirements to a threshold of $2,000,000, I feel the situation can only get worse. As one of the contact staff recently commented, the group leaders are too busy to look at a deal until the deadline for executing it has practically arrived, and because of time or marketing "constraints", will approve the loan without fully understanding the risks, relying very heavily on the judgment of the contact officer–in theory, the group leader or division head makes the credit decision; in practice, that decision is made by the contact officer. If you combine this with an increase in marketing pressure and a decline in credit skills, the potential for problems is substantial. If you add the attempt on the part of the contact staff to "handle their own problems", you multiply the risk because the attention required in "problem handling" reduces the time available for following the loan portfolio and for analyses of new situations, with the result that the problem does not get handled well and the portfolio is subject to undetected deterioration.

I don't know whether it is work load, administrative limitations or the ability of the Senior Analyst, but I feel that the quality of the credit analyses has slipped materially and that some of the basic fundamentals of credit analyses are being overlooked. Some read more like a sales promotion rather than an objective analysis. I don't know where the problem lies, but I think that something should be done about it.

While I realize that we may not want to take the step, I feel that serious consideration should be given to having credit officers assigned to lending groups when their outstandings reach certain thresholds. The credit officer would presumably report to the division head. He would be responsible to him for the credit worthiness of loans not requiring LAC approval.

As you know, there has been a growing tendency for group leaders to try to retain responsibility for handling workout loans on the theory of marketing image, industry expertise, etc. As a practical matter, the industry groups were established for the purpose of market penetration rather than for the purpose of developing credit specialties. From analyses of the loans which have been classified #5's, I think that it is clear that the credit skills have not developed and that, if anything, the industry specialty aura has tended to cloud judgment rather than enhance it. Illustrations of this would be our shipping loans, Thor, Enterprise Radio, London Energy Group and the Essex Company as an offhand sample. This, incidentally, is not an unusual kind of development. Looking back on our own experience, our floor plan loans to dealers were somehow "different" and not subject to the laws of cause and effect. I don't know that Ken Jackson ever did understand that if you finance 100% of a new car for a dealer and the dealer sells it taking back a trade whose value is in excess of his gross profit on the sale of the new car, you either end up out of trust or financing a used car inventory as soon as the dealer's capital is no longer sufficient to carry his own used cars. Of course, the most recent and most expensive experience we have had is in our shipping group's involvement in "world ship financing" while in reality financing transportation equipment for individuals who didn't have sufficient capital to meet basic working capital requirements.

As of May 31 our controlled loans totaled $134.3 million. Of this amount, $26.6 or 20% was handled by the International Division, $9.6 or 7% was handled by the South Group, $29.3 or 22% was handled by the Commercial Finance Group and $68.8 or 51% was handled by the Controlled Loan Department. While I know that these are all exceptions to the general policy, it raises real questions in the minds of the lending departments as to the enforceability of the policy, if for no other reason than that any policy which is waived 50% of the time on the face of it is not particularly strongly enforced. It gives rise to the argument of "If they are not subject to the policy, why should I be?" I might

> comment here that the shipping loans being handled in the International Division by John Dorman were established as a trial balloon due to the complexities of ship financing involving foreign ownership and lawyers centered primarily in London and Greece. The people following the bulk of these loans with John Dorman were responsible for either having approved or made the loans in the first place, and the same misguided practices which led to undue exposure to begin with were carried out after the loans were classified as workouts. I think the mystique of dealing with shipping situations has been grossly over-played, and the fact that we are financing basic transportation equipment over-looked. The financial results of the efforts to date strongly indicate that the experiment was unsuccessful. The bottom line losses and expenses against recoveries and loan repayments strongly suggest to me that we try another tack despite protestations by Bill Marshall and others involved that a better job could not have been done. I would strongly recommend that shipping loans which are basic commercial loans not involving any sovereign risk be transferred back to the responsibility of the Controlled Loan Department so that they can be properly handled. This could be effected very simply by having Dorman report to Perrault rather than Marshall.

Despite the clarity of the serious issues regarding portfolio management, no meaningful action was taken to address them. Driscoll clearly chose not to exercise his authority, deigning to reign but not rule.

Business philosophy in this country seems to be that bigger is better and that growth in sales volume is synonymous with business success. To some extent, this is the case; growth in many cases is indeed a measure of corporate success. On the other hand, a rate of growth that clearly surpasses that of other competitors in traditional markets should be a clear signal to management that their "success" in the marketplace may be attributable to a compromise of traditional standards and should be carefully analyzed to determine whether the growth is really due to better marketing or whether it is actually being attained at the expense of sound business practice. When competition in traditional markets becomes heated and emphasis on stock performance becomes an overriding concern—in fact, at any time—the subordination of basic bank management and bank-lending principles for the sake of growth is ultimately a disastrous strategy.

THE END IS NEAR
http://www.endnear.com

Entering New Markets

How to Grow in the Face of Existing Competition

For all practical purposes, large commercial banks provide identical services in their market areas. Given the bank coverage, there is no part of the country that could be considered "underbanked." In addition, due to the similarity of banking services, banking relationships, once established, tend to be stable. This raises some serious questions about how to enter new market areas in the face of existing competition. The soundest strategy, from a credit standpoint, is probably to purchase or merge with existing banks in the area where possible and to expand the business through their existing networks. In the late 1970s, BNE decided to expand its lending operations outside its traditional geographic marketing areas and decided to do so de novo.

Customer Service Offices and Loan Production Offices were opened in various parts of the country to generate all types of commercial loans. Personnel in these offices had no lending authority but would present loan proposals for approval and execution in Massachusetts. The Customer Service Offices concentrated on commercial finance opportunities (loans secured by the assignment of accounts receivable, inventories, and fixed assets in many cases). The Loan Production Offices concentrated on real estate loans for the most part, but on occasion generated other types of commercial lending opportunities. The hazards overlooked or played down at the time of opening were those associated with persuading customers of other banks to switch from their established relationships to an out-of-area unknown bank. Staffing of the offices presented another problem: why should a banker who was well regarded and well established in his present institution switch? What enticement could be given? The answer to the first question of why the customer should switch was answered by offering incentives the existing lenders would not, such as easier credit standards or lending against collateral unacceptable to the existing lender or other local lending institutions. For example, some of the commercial finance loans were made by including real estate as part of the collateral borrowed against where local lenders would not. When some of these loans went bad, the real estate was found to be contaminated to the point where the real estate was abandoned rather than foreclosed. Another enticement was to offer a more competitive interest rate, but this option was not used out of concern for "bottom line" erosion. The problem of getting well-experienced and respected personnel was met by offering salaries equivalent to those offered in Boston, salaries considerably higher than those being paid in the areas being entered. Even so, the skills of many of the personnel attracted by bank's hired headhunter to the Customer Service Offices as managers and account officers were deficient from the standpoints of administrative capacity, risk assessment capability, and educational background; they were a far cry from those of their counterparts in Boston. The lack of skills was thought to be ameliorated by the fact that none of the personnel in the Customer Service Offices or LPOs had any lending authority. This lack of authority presumably served two purposes as it was supposed to limit the credit risk to that which met with Boston standards, and there may have been no requirement to report to the various states as a company doing business there since all of the loans granted were technically made in Boston. On the other hand, one had to wonder about the impression customers and prospects were left with after having been called upon by some of the bank's representatives.

Creating Impressions in a New Geographic Market

While working for Irving Trust Company in New York during the 1960s and 1970s, we lived in Armonk where IBM had its headquarters and where many IBM employees lived. It was interesting that IBM seemed to have a dress code for its people, not only in the Armonk headquarters, but also for its salesmen and others in the field. The purpose, of course, was to convey an impression of consistent professionalism throughout the organization. The Bank of New England would have been well advised to emulate that intent in their selection and training of the people who represented them. As mentioned above, many of the Customer Service Office personnel employed by Commercial Finance did not seem to be "cut from the same cloth" as their counterparts in Boston. One individual who comes to mind was referred to as Preacher Bob when he came to Boston to give a presentation to a loan approval committee (either senior or divisional). His style of presentation was akin to that of giving a sermon, complete with emotional gestures. While there was nothing inherently wrong with the content of some of his presentations, his mannerisms, mispronounced words, and rather whiney tone of voice often resulted in laughter and derisive remarks about Preacher Bob after he had left the room. He clearly did not have the personal respect of any member of the committee or his Boston counterparts that he perhaps deserved. One had to wonder if he were regarded as the laughingstock of the Customer Service Offices by those in Boston, how could those upon whom he called while representing the bank have any different impression? What impression did they get of the institution for which he worked?

Not surprisingly, for the most part, things did not develop as planned. For years the eroded credit standards in the Customer Service Offices, as a group, resulted in net losses. The results of real estate operations centered in Philadelphia took longer to surface than the commercial finance problems due to their longer draw-down nature but ultimately played a significant role in the failure of the bank. As will be commented on later, a $140 million leveraged buyout loan brought in by our Loan Production Office in Chicago resulted in the bank's becoming the lead lender and later produced the largest single loss in the bank's history along with very unfavorable commentary in local newspapers.

Competing Through Lower Rates and Increased Risk

Entry into new markets may be accomplished through other means as well as geographic expansion. The new markets BNE chose to enter included types of financing not previously offered by the bank, such as shipping, alternate energy sources, fuel distribution and utilities, communications, and leveraged buyouts, to mention a few. Unfortunately, the prospects successfully solicited were, for the most part, the marginal producers; taking these customers on again put business growth ahead of business quality and proper risk management.

Just as with entry into new geographical markets, entry into established markets not previously served is generally accomplished in either of two ways, the first being to lend to established companies at an interest rate lower than that being offered by existing banks, and the second is to be willing to accept higher levels of risk through lending to those fringe players other banks ignore, accepting collateral others will not, or lending more against collateral than competing banks. Unfortunately, the decision to accept the higher risks rather than to lower interest rates ultimately resulted in heavy losses.

The greatest weakness in these failed attempts to broaden the lending base of the bank was a lack of real understanding of the risks involved in the various types of loans being made. Rather than taking the time and effort to get a clear understanding of the risks through independent and objective industry analysis, the Credit Department analysts depended almost entirely on the account officers (many of whom had weak credit skills). What many analysts were led to believe was considered routine financing or technology was really new and unproven. In other cases, basic research on the principals of the borrower would have revealed a lack of experience in the industry, a lack of proven management ability, or a history of unsuccessful ventures. While having managed a company or other commercial enterprise that has filed for protection under the Bankruptcy Code may not be evidence of dishonesty on the part of the principals, it is clearly good evidence of a lack of managerial ability and, as such, a clear warning sign of increased risk.

Lending to Poorly Understood Fringe Markets

There were also risks involved in diversifying the nature of the customer base to include industries not traditionally financed by the bank, such as the fuel industry. As with new geographical market entry, the easiest place to penetrate is the fringe borrower. Pressure to penetrate the market can result in loans that really tax common sense. An example follows.

The national accounts group, established to handle and solicit banking opportunities with large corporations, formed a special group to solicit the traditional energy market ostensibly to try to penetrate the larger energy producers nationwide. The acknowledged established players in this market, by and large, already have well-established banking connections; getting them to start a new relationship is very difficult. The result is that the penetrable segment of the market is largely a peripheral one populated by marginal operations or by "special situations." One such situation offered to us was a tax shelter deal put together by two men who once worked in one of the trust departments in town. In their new firm, they had persuaded a group of their former bank customers to put up the minimum amount of equity required for the purchase of a portable mill to be used in separating coal from culm piles at an old coal-mining site in Pennsylvania. Bank of New England agreed to finance the balance of the purchase price. The culm piles, incidentally, were formed when strip coal-mining operators discarded surface earth removed in order to expose solid veins of coal for extraction. Typically, the soil discarded included some coal, although at then-current coal prices, not enough for the strip miner to consider it worth the effort to separate from the earth being discarded. The portable mill was designed to facilitate the separation of the coal from culm piles using a series of conveyor belts and other equipment. In addition, due to its portability, the mill could be transported from one mining site to another after the coal in one culm pile had been exhausted. Due to the national emphasis on domestic energy production, there were tax advantages for the owners in addition to the revenues generated from the sale of the reclaimed coal.

Even on the surface, the operation appeared to be very marginal. The proposed loan was well over $1 million—large enough to require presentation to the Senior Loan Approval Committee. During the presentation, enough questions were raised to prompt the comment that the operation appeared to have about as much relevance to the coal industry as a rag picker had to the textile industry. Nonetheless, the loan was approved. The mill was described as being portable because it was bolted together rather than welded but, in fact, turned out to be several stories high and bolted to a thick six-foot cement slab the size of a football field. In any event, the operation was never a success. To top it off, the state of Pennsylvania (and perhaps the Environmental Protection Agency or EPA) decreed that all strip mining left scars on the countryside, and therefore, all operators had to take part in returning the site to as near to its original condition as possible and would have to do so at their own expense. Lest the bank be classified as an operator and be forced to return the property to its original condition, the property was abandoned, mill and all. The "portable" mill was sold for scrap by the state. The investors got their tax benefit in a way they had not contemplated: they had a substantial total loss.

Other attempts at innovation were not innovative; they simply lacked common sense. One such example was a loan proposal brought to the SLAC to lend to a middle-market fuel farm operator. After the proposal had been introduced by the account officer, the district head proudly stated that the account officer had shown innovative thinking that paid off in the company's selection of our bank as opposed to competing institutions. When pressured as to exactly what the innovative approach had been, the officer admitted that he had offered to make the loan unsecured, whereas the competition wanted collateral for the loan. The loan was approved by the chairman of the SLAC. As things ultimately turned out, the management of the company began speculating in the oil futures market, the market went against them, the losses were severe, and the unsecured loan was transferred to the Controlled Loan Department for disposition. The bank's loss was inevitable.

International Loans

Lending to Those in Need

The following comments on international loans are confined to those loans with cross border risk (i.e., dollar loans made in the United States to borrowers in foreign countries as opposed to local currency loans made to local borrowers by foreign branches of US banks). "Sovereign risk" loans are those with guaranteed government support, and "private sector" loans are those dependent upon the credit strength of the borrower without government backing.

During the global oil crisis of the 1970s, the Middle Eastern oil-producing countries preferred to be paid in US dollars because of the worldwide acceptance the dollar enjoyed and the limited acceptance of the currencies of the poorer oil-importing countries. As a result, some institutions voiced increasing concerns that the volume of US dollars owned by the oil-producing countries was growing too large. To explain the issue and allay the concerns among the bank's staff, the Economics Department at Irving Trust Company put on a slide presentation for all department heads. The economist doing the presentation pointed out very clearly that there was nothing to be concerned about because the US financial institutions were efficiently "recycling" the petrodollars. In short, as dollars were paid for oil, the oil producers would return the dollars to the United States as a safe haven (invested in US government securities for the most part), and those dollars would then be loaned to countries that needed dollars to pay for oil, thus "recycling" the dollars. What was not answered by the economist, however, was the question of how countries that were already short on dollars due to a lack of exports of their own would ever be able to repay the United States the loans they received in order for them to buy oil from oil-producing countries. The countries most in need were those whose trade with the United States was the most limited. In a broad sense, logic would dictate that the problem was exacerbated rather than alleviated by the process. It was really a humanitarian effort by the United States because the countries needed the oil, and the Arab countries neither needed the oil importers' products nor would they accept their currencies in payment. A large portion of the debt would ultimately have to be forgiven.

Lending Based on Dubious Data

International loans made by Bank of New England were all handled by the International Division, as they are in most banks with any degree of international exposure. Most of the private-sector loans were to financial institutions, including banks, finance companies, and leasing companies. The ability to pay of the vast majority of the international borrowers was naturally affected by the political and economic conditions in the countries in which they operated, as well as by their ability to obtain the dollars with which to refinance or repay their obligations as they came due. The International Division also made and handled shipping loans, but these were far less impacted by cross-border conditions.

A credit analysis was required for approval of International Division loans, and the division had its own credit department to perform this function. Countries were analyzed periodically, analyses focusing on refunding capacity as indicated by political stability, economic trends, strategic importance, foreign reserves, and balance of payments data. Most of the analyses consisted of gathering economic statistics published by the various governments from agencies and firms specializing in the collection of such data, gleaning information from various publications to obtain a feel for the political atmosphere and economic progress, and summarizing the countries' prospects. Much of the data analyzed was generally about a year old because it took so long to get it. Therefore, country analyses often were heavily based on material that may not have been a valid indicator of existing conditions. As a consequence, normal analytical techniques and requirements applied to commercial lending were not applied. The process and the product had severe limitations, but for years it was felt to be all that was needed. In times of rapid economic and social change, however, it not only lost its utility, but also could send the wrong message of financial strength.

Musical Chairs: Lending Based on Refunding

The repayment history of international loans masked the underlying risks of the transactions and the fact that, with the exception of genuine trade transaction financing backed by letters of credit, banks had become collectively dependent upon their own willingness to continue to provide loans for debt repayment. Without further loans, repayment would be severely impaired. David Rockefeller, chairman of the Chase Manhattan Bank, in addressing the Economic Club of New York in the late 1970s, complained that press criticism of the LDC (less-developed countries) loans was due to their failure to understand that "these loans are meant to be repaid from refunding." The fact that he overlooked, however, was that these loans were totally dependent upon the borrowers' ability to refinance with institutions engaged in similar financings, an essential participant being the Chase Manhattan Bank. He apparently saw nothing wrong in the Chase Manhattan Bank being an essential link in an incestuous refunding group, which was expected to be the source of repayment of its members' loans. Mr. Rockefeller's comment prompted one of the guests, a corporate attorney from International Telephone and Telegraph Company (ITT), to ask me, "If you keep refunding, how do you know when the loan is bad? Do you wait until the music stops to find there is no chair?" As a case in point, page 7 of the February 9, 2005, issue of *The Christian Science Monitor* carried an article headlined, "Argentina Plays Chicken with Foreign Investors." Essentially, Argentina had given holders of $100 billion of its debt until February 25 to settle for $30 billion—thirty cents on the dollar—and many debt holders found that there was, indeed, no chair when the music stopped.

International and Commercial Lending Inexperience

With few exceptions, officers in the International Division had good contacts and international calling experience but very limited commercial-lending skills. Private sector financial statements were often submitted in the language and currency of the borrower and prepared by local accountants who may or may not have followed accounting principles generally accepted in the United States. These reports generally were submitted late, and many were further delayed by the need for translation into English. Interim financial statements were rarely submitted. Financial statements submitted by financial institutions tend to be more consistent within countries, but the accounting practices, portfolio reporting, and delay in presentation weaken the validity of any conclusions one may draw. Compounding the issues, country analysis did not utilize the kind of financial-analysis training most credit analysts receive, and since most international credit analysts did not have extensive commercial-credit experience, commercial-credit analysis skills tended to get rusty from lack of use. While the number of private-sector commercial-lending opportunities was fairly small and tended to be concentrated in financial institutions, the quality of the credit analysis suffered due to the lack of both data and experience. For example, it was and is still routine for domestic-credit analysts to deduct from the net worth of a borrower any "appraisal surplus" that appears in the net worth section of the balance sheet as accounting practices in the United States generally require the statements to reflect the assets at the lower of cost or market (there might be an exception if the assets of a financial institution include appreciated marketable securities, but other assets do not fall into that category). On the other hand, foreign financial institutions borrowing dollar-denominated debt will translate that debt into domestic currencies for statement presentation. When the domestic currency falls in value against the dollar (which happens frequently), the debt reflected on the balance sheet of the borrower increases due to the change in exchange rate; but if the assets acquired with the US dollar–denominated debt are carried in domestic currency, there is no concomitant increase in value of the assets. Since financial institutions (banks and finance companies) are often fairly highly leveraged, it does not take a big drop in the exchange rate to wipe out the institution's capital. In order not to show a deficit capital base, the institutions and their accountants often reflect their fixed assets (i.e., buildings, facilities, and other fixed assets) at an increased appraised/market value rather than at cost, thus reflecting a positive equity position that would otherwise be negative. The increase in appraised value is carried as appraisal surplus in the capital section of the balance sheet. The International Division Credit Department found this practice perfectly acceptable even though a domestic analyst would have found the borrower insolvent.

The ability of the bank to appreciate the true risk in their international lending practices was undermined by several factors, some unique to Bank of New England and others common to the industry at that time. International and other "specialty" lending tend to assume a curious aura or mystique that intentionally and effectively implies that it is beyond the ken of lenders and analysts outside the group. The "separatism" built around foreign lending somehow made it acceptable to make lending decisions based on information that was stale, often questionable, and seldom complete and where repayment was frequently completely dependent upon the borrower's ability to refinance (or "refund") at maturity. Amazingly, the credit policy officers at Bank of New England went along with the practice for years, and most reviews of international nonshipping loans were perfunctory at best. Another factor was the excellent repayment record of foreign loans. For years the bulk of international lending was sovereign risk and the losses were trifling, primarily due to ease of refunding. A third factor was the difficulty in getting a sufficient amount of accurate information in a timely manner so that financial deterioration was not readily determined.

Walking Out on Common Sense

One exception to the "go along to get along" behavior was Hugh Taylor, who, as Credit Policy Officer in 1986, sought to have the international loan portfolio reviewed in a conventional manner. The loan review was held with the head of the International Division, his Senior Credit Officer, the head of Loan Review, the Credit Policy Officer, the Loan Review Department Vice President assigned to the International Division review, and the SVP of Loan Control. The loans to be reviewed were from borrowers in Mexico and Latin America. When the weaknesses in the credits and the analyses began to be pointed out, the head of the International Division protested, finally standing up and shouting that we simply did not understand that these were not loans but investments that were fully expected to be refinanced rather than repaid in the manner of domestic commercial loans and were meant to provide an income stream. The Credit Policy Officer stood up and shouted back that they were supposed to be bank loans and not long-term investments and that they were not supported by the credit analyses; the International Division Senior Credit Officer stood up and shouted that he knew credit and that the loans were good. The meeting ended, unresolved, when the division manager and his senior credit officer walked out of the meeting. The division manager attended no more loan review meetings, and his senior credit officer attended only those to do with the shipping portfolio, leaving the International Division represented by the head of the International Division Credit Department. The division manager was partially right in describing the loans as investments because they could only be paid through refinancing and could not be repaid in any other manner at maturity. His Senior Credit Officer was wrong—the loans were very weak and were not supported by any reasonable credit standard for commercial loans. On December 31, 1985, the bank held $447 million in foreign loan and leases, and by December 31, 1987, that total had increased to $518 million. The bank charged off $192 million (roughly 37%) of International Division loans in 1988 (not counting the substantial losses incurred in the shipping portfolio). While some of the loans reviewed that day bore a superficial resemblance to loans and lines of credit extended to domestic finance and leasing companies, changes in exchange rates made the domestic currency fall in relation to the dollar, virtually eliminating any capital base. In addition, the ability of the borrowers to obtain dollars for repayment of dollar debt was almost entirely dependent on the ability to refinance the dollar-denominated debt with another lender. The risk, although unacceptable, was simply ignored.

The experience points out the dangers of allowing one's credit principles to be subordinated externally to the herd mentality ("Everybody is doing it") and internally to pressures for increased loan volume, both domestic and foreign. It also demonstrates the risk an organization assumes when management loses sight of the objective of greater corporate good by catering to market pressures and desire for internal harmony rather than to objective operational review and discipline.

Given all of the above, the enthusiasm with which the banks embraced international loans may well be explained as being due to a shortage of alternative lending opportunities and a desire for growth in size and earnings combined with a lack of a real understanding of the underlying risks. Too many banks became involved and collectively provided too much of the credit, which should have been provided, if at all, by international governmental agencies rather than by private banks. This is particularly true in the case of loans that were used to fund deficits rather than trade transactions or industrial development.

Measurements of Management Effectiveness

Growing Pains

There is no room for complacency or weakness in bank management. In companies with ineffective management, critical, objective internal evaluations of performance are often missing and often politically motivated and subjective. As demonstrated by Bank of New England, the consequences can be severe. There are, however, warning signs for the effective manager, warning signs that should be recognized through an objective corporate-performance evaluation. In the early 1980s, the Boston chapter of Robert Morris Associates held a meeting at which a bank analyst from the firm of Keefe, Bruyette & Woods was the featured speaker. At one point in his address, he mentioned that, in his experience, he found that a bank growing faster than its peers generally ran into trouble. Outsiders most often evaluate an organization's management through a comparative analysis of its performance as reflected in company growth patterns and financial performance. Given the similarity in bank services, it only makes sense for management to investigate thoroughly the reasons for their institution's apparently unusual competitive success and to make sure that a growth rate in excess of industry patterns is not being achieved at the expense of sound lending practices. At Bank of New England, the warning signs had been there for some time. This was pointed out in the memo to the Credit Policy Officer dated October 26, 1982. That memo appears later in this chapter and was the first of many such memos.

Management Mettle Fatigue

In his article entitled "The Scent of Failure and the Use of Risk Analysis,"[5] Haig J. Boyadjian cites a "fatigue risk model" that he developed for use in the assessment of prospective borrower management. While it was primarily designed for rating commercial businesses, this mode is a useful tool in assessing the effectiveness of the management of any organization. Clear indicators of management inadequacy (what he terms the management metal fatigue risk) include frequent reorganizations and executive reshuffling, redefinition of objectives, and dominance of organizational issues over business priorities. Bank of New England evidenced all of these symptoms. For example, the credit policy officer was changed on an average of every two years, each time as a result of more extensive personnel reshufflings; the Boston bank had three presidents and five credit policy officers in nine years. Frequent reorganizations occurred, such as among the lending groups to form new "specialties" with new objectives, and within operating areas and in combinations and regroupings within the affiliated/subsidiary banks. These ostensibly were made to become more efficient or to cover the market better.

"Senior Vice-President Buffington reporting, sir. Requests permission to advance and be recognized."

management's "mettle" fatigue is blaming or finger-pointing, such as the comments of Walter Connolly (chairman of Bank of New England Corp.) and Richard Driscoll (Chairman of Bank of New England, NA) quoted in the April 4, 1989, issue of the *Boston*

Globe. Connolly and Driscoll said that the problems then beginning to surface were limited to Bank of New England, North and that the management and lending staff of the Bank of New England, North was inadequate. As a practical matter, the bank in question and its predecessors had been subsidiaries of Bank of New England for some time, enough time to assess the quality of its management. If they did so, obviously they failed to anticipate what was coming.

Diversion and Avoidance of Responsibility

The dominance of structural issues over business priorities was pointed out in the first chapter; the boxes in the organization chart were filled, and the responsibilities were therefore presumed to be properly discharged. Warning signs to the contrary and operating deficiencies that were clearly pointed out in Loan Review reports and other memos to the Credit Policy Officer were systematically ignored, and the increasing risks stemming from the lack of managerial and administrative skill on the part of managers went unchecked.

The parallel of conditions at Bank of New England in 1985 (prior to the merger with Connecticut Bank and Trust) and Continental Illinois National Bank and Trust, which failed in 1984, were alarming. A memo written to the Credit Policy Officer at Bank of New England in March 1985 reads as follows:[6]

Bank of New England
Memorandum

To: Robert T. McAlear, Senior Vice President

From: Charles B. M. Douglas, Senior Vice President

Re:

Date: March 29, 1985

I read through the report of the special Litigation Committee of the Board of Continental Illinois and found that the conclusions drawn were largely self-serving. They were also a further symptom of some of the problems which Continental had. Two of the problems which are apparent are probably intertwined, but I would classify them as follows:

1. The management of the Bank was unable to distinguish where delegation of authority ended and abdication of responsibility began.

2. The management of the Bank had put into place very effective management control systems *which because of their existence* gave such a feeling of security that management refused to acknowledge that subordinates were not reacting appropriately—in short, they intellectually turned management over to the system, leaving the real management function void.

Each of these problems is of concern because to some degree I think that we are seeing them arise here.

1. The first of these is a particularly sensitive issue for senior management but it should not be, and should be addressed squarely rather than in the ineffective manner in which Continental reacted. The insidious manner in which it spreads can make it particularly devastating in its pervasiveness. In the case of Continental, the problem is exemplified by the fact that prolonged interdepartmental accusations and excuses misdirected the focus of attention away from the real issues of credit soundness to those of operational efficiency and procedures. The lending staff's tactic was successful in diverting responsibility with the result that operating procedures were minimally changed and the issues of credit soundness were not really addressed until it was too late. There are many other examples of the lack of assuming proper responsibility when it was known that established procedures were not being adhered to—the problems were always somebody else's to correct.

   Some of these issues may have arisen because of confusion between senior management on the one hand and lending groups on the other as to the amount of responsibility and authority which had actually been delegated. While we would like to believe that that does not happen here, our loan approval process by its nature lends itself to conflict. Psychologically you cannot separate responsibility from authority without creating an atmosphere of confusion in which nobody *really* feels accountable. For example, LAC has approved certain loans against its better judgment based on its understanding that the lending group was fully responsible—had the members of LAC been held accountable for the results, many of those loans would not have been made. In some cases, large losses have been sustained, but management has taken no visible action to discipline anyone for the loss. I am not suggesting that any "one" be disciplined, but rather pointing out that by inaction *no one is seen as being held responsible* if loans go bad, and those precedents are going to be almost impossible to overcome equitably. Our loan proposals have become much larger on the average, the complexity and leverage are greater. Has the time come for LACs to take the *responsibility* for the loans they approve and for them to act as real approval bodies? Should the lending officers be held strictly accountable for *prudent handling* of all of their loans? Should credit approval by higher authority absolve those beneath it?

It may be argued that a committee cannot effectively be "blamed" for a bad decision, but that really is not the issue. Committee approval would in fact say: "This makes good business sense and the risks are acceptable. If the lending officer's behavior has been prudent and a loss sustained, it will be regarded as a cost of doing business."

2. It would be foolish to argue that firm, established systems and procedures are not necessary guidelines in the conduct of any business. It is equally foolish to argue that systems should remain static while the business evolves. The procedures which were put in place in this bank many years ago were effective for many years in maintaining control in spite of substantial growth. On the other hand, volume in many areas has grown to the point where the systems need reform. I feel that there are many cases which indicate that we are relying more on procedures simply because they are there rather than on the concepts which lay behind their formulation. We are stressing too much form over substance. For example:

a. We have had a term loan compliance procedure which was to have been followed in the Credit Department. For many years the only term loan compliance check which has been provided occurs when credits are analyzed. The #427 Group Term Loan Report lists all of the term loans on the CML [a computerized report] and is produced on an off-quarter end, i.e. January, April, July and October. One copy is produced, it is sent to the Credit

Department—and thrown away. There are no quarterly checks on compliance with covenants, and fiscal requirements are reviewed at analysis time—no analysis, no check. The fact that the procedure is there is not really a source of comfort.

b. Employees not actually recruited for the management trainee program and who subsequently join it sign on for credit analysis for an additional year. While this is not a bad policy, to adhere to it blindly (as was the case with Ruth Brass) is another example of absolute insistence on form over substance.

c. The Credit Department training personnel appear to be trying to establish themselves as an avant-garde analytical group, with the reputation as such being the objective. Hence the LIFO/FIFO fiasco and unusual reconciliation exercise on each of the P&L spreads which few, *if any*, contact officers understand. Wouldn't time and effort be better spent in developing real skills, such as real estate expertise.

There are many other examples which can be cited.

Aside from the loss of effective control which can result from emphasizing form too much and substance not enough, the practice tends to have a demoralizing effect on personnel. It can become a haven in which the ineffective and insecure take refuge, and it leads to an impression of senseless inflexibility and the frustrations that come from trying to deal with non-functioning but stated policy. The frustrations can lead to the more able and less patient becoming discouraged or simply leaving.

Our policy currently calls for the Senior Loan Officer as being the only officer in the bank who can approve the classification of a loan as a #6. This policy was waived in its entirety by Peter McCormick from 1978 through 1981 when Robert Elliott was given the responsibility and authority by Peter. I do not know when the policy was originally adopted, but clearly the loan portfolio and the average size of individual loans was smaller and the quality of our loans was higher than it is today. Our loans are over $3 billion, 60% rated #4 or #5, the average loan a multiple of what it was a year ago and the leverage as indicated by the ratings considerably higher. It appears on the surface to be an anachronism that a bank of this size requires, by a policy, that the Senior Loan Officer be required to agree that a bad situation is bad enough to call it bad. The statement of this policy has often resulted in a procedure of negotiation between the Loan Review OIC and division heads rather than one of objective classification. Also, psychologically the Loan Review OIC is less apt to call a spade a spade until he is absolutely sure that he will not be overridden. In some cases the delays can be costly. It would appear to make more sense to

> also grant the OIC Loan Review the explicit authority to rate any loan a #6 at his discretion. If the Loan Review OIC and his staff are not competent enough to do the job, who is? He should have the authority to insure that the rating system's integrity is maintained because it is part of the job. The Credit Department has not assigned a #6 rating to any credit in over two years. It appears that the real issue may not be whether the loan is good or bad but rather where a bad loan is to be handled. If this is that case, it should be kept in mind that the Loan Review function and the Controlled Loan function are entirely different, and that there is a provision in existing policy for the President or the Senior Loan Officer to grant an exemption so that the loan can be handled anywhere he directs—CML, Chapter 14, Section 4.A.
>
> [CBMD]/Emc

Unfortunately, McAlear was transferred to manage the Commercial Finance Department soon after assuming the position of Credit Policy Officer, and the issues raised in the memo went unaddressed.

Turf Wars

Prior to the CBT merger with Bank of New England Corporation, BNENA competed with other banks in the New England market, but with the CBT acquisition, the competitive slant changed. The issue of bank dominance within the corporation became an underlying issue that was never resolved and that was responsible for a good deal of the emphasis on what appeared on the surface as growth for growth's sake—ostensibly the one with the most loans would be dominant and would "win." The chairman, Walter Connolly, felt that proper management was patterned after a military structure. The problem was that he did not have the leadership qualities necessary to manage a large and aggressive institution effectively. He apparently had been, however, a good-enough politician to achieve the height of management at Connecticut Bank and Trust, perhaps because of the manner in which that bank had grown. It was, essentially, the result of many acquisitions of smaller banks engaged in what was referred to as retail banking. Being considerably smaller than the acquirer, their managements were automatically subordinated to the CBT management in Hartford. When it came to the "merger of equals" between CBT and Bank of New England, however, the power struggle for dominance was a far cry from the one CBT had enjoyed in its prior mergers. Bank of New England, Boston was supposed to be stronger in commercial credit by virtue of its long history as a wholesale bank and was said to have the credit policy responsibility for the corporation. That decision (and many others that allocated responsibility on a corporate basis) was never effectively implemented due to the continual vying for dominance between the Bank of New England, Boston on the one hand and CBT on the other and the unwillingness or inability of either management to address the issues objectively. This fruitless struggle for dominance diverted management attention from the real job at hand: ensuring adequate controls in a changing and very competitive market.

One of the consequences of internal competition was the heavy emphasis on loan-portfolio growth at Bank of New England, Boston. Since the real estate market was getting very active, the easiest and fastest way to grow the portfolio was an aggressive pursuit of large commercial real estate loans, and the easiest way to get the loans was to weaken credit standards, which the bank proceeded to do. Even though the loan portfolio was the largest asset on the corporate balance sheet and the source of its growth and majority of its income, Connolly had a limited understanding of credit risk. Given that his responsibility as chairman was that of overseeing the effective management of both CBT and BNENA, it was essential for him to have in place the presidents of the affiliated banks, who in turn could perform their management functions in an effective manner. This required that he understand the basic characteristics of the loan portfolios in at least the largest of the affiliated banks, which he did not have. In addition, he was either unable or unwilling to prevent the destructive political struggling between affiliates. Connolly's lack of basic understanding of commercial lending is illustrated by an incident that occurred at a meeting to discuss the status of the workout loans and proposed loan charge-offs at BNE, Boston. Present at the meeting were all of the account officers in the Controlled Loan Department, the head of Loan Review (Larry Kelley), the chairman of the bank

(Richard Driscoll), the chairman of the corporation (Walter Connolly), the president of the bank (Thomas Wilson), the incoming head of Loan Control (David Nordby), and myself. Connolly took the chairmanship of the meeting. The first loan up for discussion was a $25 million loan to A. J. Lane, a large commercial real estate developer that had filed for bankruptcy. The account officer began by saying that the loan was on nonaccrue status (the bank was not accruing interest on the loan). Connolly interrupted him, leaning across the table toward him, punctuating his words by pointing a finger at him, and saying in an angry voice, "You told me that this loan would not be put on nonaccrue!"

The account officer was taken aback and denied having spoken with Connolly. I broke in and pointed out that the company was in bankruptcy and that it would be up to the court to approve any payments. Connolly glared at me and said, "I'll have the last word in this!" With that, he looked down at his papers and shuffled them for a minute before getting up abruptly and stalking out of the room. There was silence for a minute or so, then Driscoll got up, picked up his papers without looking at anyone, and walked out. So Wilson got up, looked around, and said, "Well, I guess the meeting is over." The purpose of the meeting (to discuss the quarterly charge-offs) was never met. Executive leadership was nowhere to be seen.

This lack of leadership had been prevalent for some time within the Bank of New England. The following memo was written in October 1982 to the Credit Policy Officer; while it is directed toward the apparent weaknesses at Bank of New England, Boston, the points are equally valid for acquisitions of smaller banks in subsequent years.[7]

Bank of New England
Memorandum
Confidential

To: Richard D. Driscoll, Executive Vice President

From: Charles B.M. Douglas, Senior Vice President

Re: Confidential Observations

Date: October 26, 1982

I thought it would be well to comment on certain areas that I have been exposed to as the head of Loan Control for approximately a year. I think that none of the points that I will cover below are new to you, and some may be somewhat colored by my relatively short perspective of one year on the job.

1. As the Bank has grown, there has been an increasing emphasis on the marketing skills of the contact staff in virtually all of the lending groups. This emphasis has resulted in a sacrifice of credit skills. This is not necessarily unhealthy nor, for that matter, is it unexpected, but I believe that it will have to be offset by certain changes in procedures if the evolution from calling credit officer

to contact officer is to be accomplished in a healthy, progressive way.

2. The credit training which the management trainees receive tends to be academic in nature and of relatively short duration, with the result that calling officers tend to forget some of the basic principles which do not apply in the specific areas to which they are currently assigned. For example, I strongly suspect that officers assigned to the International Division rapidly lose their commercial credit lending skills from lack of use, as the majority of their contacts are with institutional or sovereign risk. I suspect that some of our shipping loans might not have been made had they been viewed strictly as commercial loans secured by transportation equipment, as opposed to being somehow different because of their foreign ownership and involvement in transporting goods on the water, as opposed to over the roads or railroads.

3. The staff in our CSOs is built with an eye toward servicing lending efforts, with the result that when a problem arises which requires concentrated attention, either the problem is not given the attention it needs, or other efforts of the CSO fall behind.

CD00007

Richard D. Driscoll Page 2

October 26, 1982

To a certain degree, the same situation exists in other lending groups where loans which would normally be made by a specialized lending group, instead, are monitored out of the contact officer's desk. Collateral, in these cases, in reality serves as a general lending guideline, rather than having the same importance that it would in CFD, Equipment Finance, or Real Estate. The danger is that it tends to be viewed as a hard collateral number which can only be reliable as such if closely monitored.

The assessment of managerial skills is an ability which is not easily transferred. As a basic principle, loans are made to companies on the basis of how the people in those organizations perform. Certain members of our contact staff, I do not believe, have had enough experience to determine the managerial capabilities of the companies to whom they are offering loans. In many cases, the actual contact has been infrequent and, in most cases, limited to the financial staff of the company called upon. One has to question how much reliance should be put on the statement "the account officer has a high regard for management," which appears in almost every credit analysis.

Traditionally, managerial skills are measured analytically by objective review of financial statements. In order to provide a positive environment for a contact staff strong in marketing skills, but somewhat shy on managerial assessment and credit skills, I feel that it might be appropriate for certain of the lending groups to establish group credit officers who would have no marketing responsibilities and be directly responsible to the division head for the credit worthiness of all new loans made below the LAC requirement level. An opportune time to introduce this concept might well be when the loan level for Loan Approval Committee presentation is raised above its present level.

On the international side, it is recommended that credit training for prospective international officers be directed toward the kinds of loans which would normally be made in the International Division. The assessment of country risk is an involved procedure which may not have an established training program such as there is for general commercial lending. I would recommend that we explore the possibility of having a survey program, with institutions such as Morgan Guaranty, to try to determine the manner in which they evaluate country risk. I would also recommend a rotation for personnel between the International and Domestic Credit Departments and recommend that both credit departments report to Gordon Bennett. The switch in reporting procedure should insure that the entire analysis function remain an objective bank staff resource, rather than being under the jurisdiction of a line function.

CD00008

Richard D. Driscoll Page 3

October 26, 1982

As far as the Controlled Loan Department is concerned, its primary function of a supporting department to all lending areas should continue. By having the workout loans at CSOs the responsibility of one individual in the Controlled Loan Department, more effective monitoring progress on a day-to-day and week-to-week basis can be effected than is the case where the CSO staff has a greater responsibility both to service existing accounts completely and to generate new business. The leverage in many of the loans handled by our CSOs is such that our exposure should not be increased by diversion of the staff's attention to a workout, which, as you know, involves an incredible amount of time if it is to be done well. I expect that this same observation might well be applied to our shipping portfolio.

CBMD/nlkCD00009

Driscoll did not respond directly to any of the observations made in this memo, revealing as early as 1982 the lack of leadership that presaged the downfall of the bank.

Dominos: Failure to Manage the Managers

When Bank of New England failed in January 1991, it was the largest commercial banking failure in

New England commercial banking history and one of the largest in the history of commercial banking nationwide. As stated in the prologue, the losses to stockholders, debenture holders, and the federal government totaled approximately $5.7 billion *plus* loss of insurance coverage by the retirees and the loss of value in unexercised options.

Corporate disasters typically have a variety of root causes—specific decisions, failure to make decisions in a timely manner, failure to exercise discipline when called for—a host of actions that accumulate with fatal results. In a simplistic view, the operation of any business breaks down into a limited number of areas: marketing, production, finance, and administration. These areas are all interrelated and interdependent, and an imbalance in any one of them may result in serious problems. By far the largest percentage of corporate debacles is caused by a ripple effect: lack of proper delegation of responsibility and concomitant authority resulting in poor and inadequate managerial supervision and coordination, in turn failing to assure that all major functions are performed efficiently.

1. Marketing, of course, is the selling and distribution of the goods or services the organization provides. This includes, among other things, being aware of changes in the markets served, continual evaluation of competitive products, evaluation of the manner in which the services or products are being marketed, and evaluation of new markets for new and existing products.

2. Production is the performance of the required tasks to provide the goods or services the organization markets in a timely and cost-effective manner. This involves employment and training of qualified personnel and the use and development of proper controls and procedures. For those engaged in providing services, it includes effective cost evaluation of the services provided; for those engaged in the manufacture and sale of goods, it includes timely, cost-effective purchasing of goods and services, efficient production of manufactured goods, maintenance of an efficient distribution system to support marketing, and adequate research into product improvement and development.

3. Finance is not only the function of providing the required funds to pay for the cost of goods or services produced, the selling and administrative costs of the organization, and a return to the investors. For banks it includes the cost of raising funds to support lending activities. It also includes establishing the proper control mechanisms to make sure that all income and costs are properly recorded and allocated in a timely manner.

4. Administration is the function of coordinating all of the above functions required in the successful operation of the organization and includes that of planning for management succession and establishment of corporate

> goals and objectives. Administration is the managing of the operation, both at the division or department level as well as the management of the enterprise as a whole. It is the function of top management to "manage the managers" to *ensure that all of the responsibilities throughout the organization are being properly discharged.*

Shortly after the corporate consolidation of computer operations, Bank of New England Corporation held a senior management meeting, one of several held periodically. In attendance were the chairmen and the presidents of all of the affiliated banks and their executive vice presidents. The meeting was chaired by Walter Connolly, chairman of BNEC. The purpose of the meeting was ostensibly to discuss developments of corporate interest, including changes in policies and procedures. One of the attendees had been promoted to EVP subsequent to the prior senior management meeting, and this was his first attendance. He had prepared some comments regarding problems he had observed and areas for improvement. Before it became his turn to comment to the assembled group, the president of one of the former Conifer banks (merged into BNEC in 1986) started to speak. He began to criticize the manner in which the consolidation was being implemented and the problems that were beginning to surface as a result; the person overseeing the consolidation immediately began to disagree, and the chairman severely chastised the subsidiary president for his criticism. It was clear that criticism, however

"So, Hargrove, are we singing from the same hymnbook?"

constructive, was not welcome; the new EVP put his notes back in his pocket and remained silent. At best, differences were expected to be settled between interdependent department heads themselves, regardless of how polarized they might have become. It ignored the fact that senior management's responsibility is to ensure that all managers' goals are aligned to achieve a common corporate purpose and that any differences in perception are resolved promptly and effectively.

ITT, one of our customers at Irving Trust Company, provides an interesting contrast in management style. ITT used to hold monthly management meetings for the heads of all of its subsidiaries, rotating the meetings between Brussels and New York City. The meetings were chaired by Harold Geneen, chairman of ITT. Each of the subsidiary managers spoke about developments in their particular company. At a luncheon, I asked one of the treasury personnel whether the presentations were pretty much limited to show how well the company was doing, to which the reply was "Hell, no. Good news is fine, but you really get in trouble if you don't speak out about problems in your area. Geneen's firm requirement is that he be informed of problems because he can't make sure they are fixed if he doesn't know they exist."

Misspeaking

In the summer of 1983, a periodic ninety-day review meeting with the Loan Review Department was held with the SVP in charge of one of the lending groups and the EVP in charge of commercial banking. One of the loans was to a company known as Dual-Lite, mentioned briefly in the June 23, 1983, memo from the head of Loan Control to the Credit Policy Officer:[8]

> While the role of an agent in a multi bank credit has tended to be fairly clear and has been a desirable position to be in due to the kudos and fees which accrue to the agent bank, the nature of syndicated credits is tending to change toward marginal situations secured by receivables and other assets, as opposed to being unsecured or secured by transportation or other productive equipment. These changes in the nature of the credits bring with them an increase in responsibility that is substantial. Being an agent is indeed desirable, but I feel that our control and handling leaves a lot to be desired. I'm thinking specifically of Springfield Sugar which, as you know, is handled in [Group SVP's] area. While I am not in a position to comment on [his] administrative capabilities

> one way or the other, my direct observation of his behavior when it comes to dealing with customers or with other banks is that [he] is unwilling to take a strong dissenting position. In the case of Timex, he refused to take a strong position on our participation for fear he might alienate the Chase. In the case of Dual-Lite, it has taken him over nine months to get a security interest in the assets and he has failed to this day to get all of the terms of the security agreement settled.

The loan to Dual-Lite was unsecured in spite of the opposing recommendation that had been made at the loan review meeting over nine months prior. When questioned about what was taking so long to get security, the group SVP replied that our attorney at Choate Hall & Stewart was having problems that were taking a long time to sort out. Since I knew the firm well and had met the attorney several times, I said I would call him to see exactly what was holding things up. My call elicited some surprise. After reviewing his file on the matter, the attorney related that several months earlier, he had been given strict instructions by the account officer at BNE to discontinue all efforts to get a security interest in the assets. I immediately went to the Credit Policy Officer, Richard Driscoll, and told him that in the process of a regular ninety-day loan review, the group SVP had misstated the status of a loan that had been evidencing increasing signs of exposure. Driscoll asked me to take the matter up with the head of commercial banking and the group SVP's boss and to get back to him. When the head of commercial banking heard the truth about the Dual-Lite legal status, he called the SVP into the office and repeated what I had told him. The SVP looked at each of us and replied simply, "I misspoke." The discussion then turned to other things, and the meeting broke up. I reported back to Driscoll. His reaction was to say, "He 'misspoke'! Shit." The incident was apparently summarily forgotten.

In a broad sense, countenancing of deliberate distortion of the truth by anyone in an organization, let alone by senior officers to other senior personnel, leads to the degradation of management integrity and credibility, a loss of respect for the individuals, an increase in what is normally called destructive office politics, and loss of corporate morale and respect.

Eager Lending of Short-Term Funds for Long-Term Purposes

Another major measure of management effectiveness is the manner in which they control liquidity. There are three basic ways in which liquidity is assured. Businesses that attain their liquidity from the conversion of assets would include all manufacturing, wholesale, and retail operations; those that depend upon asset utilization would include all banks (investment of depositor and other borrowed funds), service companies, public utilities, communications companies, and those engaged in providing transportation. Businesses that earn their revenues from providing personal and business services would include brokers, lawyers, investment counselors, and a host of other businesses. Borrowing requirements differ widely, some being very dependent on financing while others may not need any outside financing at all. In the case of those that do require outside financing, liquidity must be measured differently for each type as the balance sheets and attendant ratios will reflect the type of business.

These financial dynamics, in turn, determine capital requirements and describe the pattern of the asset conversion cycle, which simply traces the conversion of cash into inventories or other assets, from there into accounts receivable, and back into cash when the receivables are paid. The pattern of asset conversion will vary depending upon the nature of the business involved. The following chart gives some examples:

Nature of the Business	**Capital Requirements**	**Pattern of the Asset Conversion Cycle**
Manufacturers of consumer products	The capital requirements are determined by the degree to which investment is required in fixed assets, *i.e.*, the plant and equipment necessary for the conversion of raw materials to finished goods. Current assets are often supported by a combination of normal trade credit and short-term working capital borrowings from banks or other lending institutions.	Funds are used to buy raw materials and to pay the costs of converting those raw materials into finished goods, which are carried in inventory; the inventories are sold to distributors, creating receivables that generally convert to cash in thirty days. From cash to inventory to cash the cycle is generally three to six months. Their financial statements will generally reflect a positive working capital position but only fair liquidity due to the investment in plant and equipment.

Wholesalers	Due to the concentration of assets in inventories rather than in fixed assets, the capital requirements are determined by the investment in warehousing facilities and delivery equipment rather than production facilities. They are also determined by the degree to which the required investment in current assets is not met by the combination of trade debt and bank borrowings.	The cycle starts with the payment to the manufacturer for goods to be carried in inventory and sold to retailers. Receivables are generally paid in 30 to 60 days, with the cycle typically lasting 60 to 120 days. Their financial statements will show positive working capital and good liquidity due to the concentration of their investment in current assets.
Retailers	The capital requirements of retailers will vary depending upon their size; retailing chains such as Wal-Mart, Sears, etc., will normally have a greater investment in facilities than will local retailers. In general, however, the capital requirements of a retailer will consist of a relatively modest investment in fixed assets and an investment that exceeds availability of trade credit and short-term loans.	They have the shortest cycle, for while they may carry inventories for a period of time, the bulk of their sales are for cash paid by the buyer or received from credit card companies. Their financial statements should reflect positive working capital and good liquidity due to the concentration of their investment in current assets.

Companies engaged in providing a physical service, such as transportation companies	Require a relatively heavy investment in equipment and a relatively small amount in inventory (largely supplies) and receivables. The capital requirements will vary depending upon the availability of long-term funding to support the investment in fixed assets, the amount of capital representing that portion of total fixed asset investment not supported by borrowed funds.	The conversion cycle is a long one, as debt used to finance the equipment is generally paid for over the expected useful life of the equipment used in providing the service. They will often have a negative working capital position (current liabilities in excess of current assets) since the entire required annual amortization of equipment debt is reflected as a current liability on the balance sheet, while the current assets contain only cash and current receivables, typically a small amount. While financial statements do not show much liquidity, the quick payment for services rendered combined with the extended repayment requirements on debt can make revolving credit arrangements a very effective form of financing.
Natural resources companies	Natural resource companies have the requirements of manufacturers in addition to having to invest heavily in land; therefore, their capital requirements normally will reflect this investment plus that percentage of their production facilities not financed by long-term debt. If their working capital requirements cannot be met by short-term borrowings, a portion of asset support also will be required in the form of capital.	Heavy investment in land and production facilities results in an extended asset conversion cycle. For example, a paper manufacturing company will have an investment in timber land. Trees are harvested, put through a pulp mill. The paper produced is then sold to distributors, with the conversion cycle from that point forward being the same as that of any other manufacturer.

Real estate developers	In theory the real estate developer uses his equity to fund the 20% to 25% of project cost required by the lender and it is incumbent on the lender to make sure that funds advanced for one project are not used, in whole or in part, to fund the equity requirement of another. If their properties are leased to tenants on a long-term basis, they can be quite heavily leveraged.	The conversion cycle typically will be six months to a year, as the equity invested in their projects and construction funds borrowed to finance the construction will not be converted back to cash until the projects are complete and are either sold or financed on a long-term basis. Their balance sheets will reflect their annual debt service as a current liability but their current assets will typically show cash plus the current month's rents receivable, resulting in a deficit working capital position.
Commercial banks	Commercial banks invest their deposits (demand and term) and funds borrowed in the open market, in loans to borrowers whose financial dynamics reflect all of the above. Commercial banks are relatively heavily leveraged and liquidity is therefore critically important. Their liquidity will depend upon the concentrations in the different types of loans within the loan portfolio. For example, brokers' loans (overnight loans to securities dealers secured by marketable securities) provide the most liquidity, followed by commercial and industrial loans—real estate construction and loans dependent upon refunding (such as many international and communications loans) provide the least and are the most vulnerable to the vagaries of their various markets.	The conversion cycle for commercial banks will depend upon the nature of their borrowers as described in the prior column. It is imperative that the percentage of the bank's portfolio concentrated in the loans with the least liquidity be carefully determined and the quality closely monitored; unlike savings banks, which may be able to sell residential mortgage loans if a need for liquidity should arise, commercial banks may have a lesser ability to convert the required amount of loans into cash, and their ability to raise additional debt or equity may be compromised.

Sources of funds range from equity investment to "funded indebtedness," or long-term debt, to trade debt and short-term bank borrowings. It is important, however, that the type of funding be appropriate for the financial dynamics of the operation. For instance, because short-term loans are often easier to get approved, it is not uncommon for eager bankers to lend short-term funds (conceptually a form of increasing working capital liquidity) for what are really long-term purposes. One of the consequences of this practice is that the short-term loans have to be renewed continually and are frequently renewed at the original amount, in effect becoming a substitute for nonamortizing long-term debt and, in some instances, a substitute for equity. Another consequence is that because short-term loans generally do not have protective covenants regarding retention of earnings, some borrowers use their borrowings as a substitute for equity and therefore do not retain their earnings. Leverage either remains constant or increases. This is common with commercial finance borrowers. Loans with these characteristics are often justly criticized by the regulators. They can also have severe consequences for the borrower for should the loans not be renewed at maturity, the borrower may well be forced to refinance the debt elsewhere at a time when refinancing may be very difficult, if not impossible, to get. Such was the case during the late 1980s and early 1990s when banks, under pressure from regulators to improve their own liquidity, refused to renew some of their borrowers' loans. Unable to find new lenders willing to refinance the debt, some borrowers went into bankruptcy, further exacerbating the bank's problems with liquidity and the regulators. (See quote from 1989 Form 10-K below.) Bank of New England allowed the concentration in the least liquid segments of its loan portfolio to rise to an unacceptably high percentage of the total; when liquidity was desperately needed to continue operations, it was not there.

Overlooking Basic Differences among Borrowers

Regardless of the source of repayment, it is the quality of management and the manner in which they manage the assets for which they are responsible that determine whether or not all indebtedness ultimately will be repaid and whether the stockholders will be adequately rewarded. For commercial banks, an assessment of borrower management is an important component of any credit analysis and any risk rating. To help ascertain the reputation of the potential borrower's management within the industry, the assessment should use all available information, involving direct, in-depth discussions with the borrower's management as well as trade investigations. Well-managed companies can finance far more easily than those with poor or mediocre management, and that ability translates to greater liquidity for the bank. An in-depth credit analysis is particularly important when the borrower is located in a market area that is new to the bank. Unfortunately, BNE credit analyses of new-market borrowers frequently relied very heavily on information provided by the account officer, often with little or no outside investigation by the bank. When high losses and a high level of nonperforming loans accumulated,

BNE was unable to meet its critical need for liquidity due to poor portfolio quality. The following is an excerpt from the Form 10-K filed as of December 31, 1989, and is an example of this type of failure.[9]

> Since the Corporation announced the significant increase in nonperforming assets and projected loss levels on December 15, 1989, there has been a decline of over $7 billion of deposits.
>
> In late January, due to deposit withdrawals, the Corporation began borrowing from the Federal Reserve Bank's discount window. Although the level of borrowings changes from day to day, and has been as high as $2.3 billion, on March 28, 1990 the federal borrowing balance was $1.7 billion. The Corporation has deposited with the Federal Reserve Bank of Boston approximately $15 billion of collateral, primarily loans of the Bank of New England banks, for these borrowings. This collateral provides a maximum of approximately $8 billion of borrowing potential at the window, although there is no assurance that the Fed would advance the maximum amount.
>
> Borrowings at the Federal Reserve Bank window may continue throughout the second quarter and into the remainder of 1990. While deposit outflow as of March 1990 had leveled off substantially from the level experienced following the January 1990 announcement which specified the extent of the 1989 loss, the Corporation's deposit base continued to decline. The future level of deposits depends upon a

number of factors, including public confidence, which are difficult to predict. As and when sales of subsidiary banks' assets are completed, management intends that proceeds will be used principally to meet deposit outflows and/or to reduce the federal borrowings.

In January 1990, the Corporation embarked on an asset disposition program encompassing the sale of non-strategic assets, loan portfolio run-off, and asset securitization. In the first quarter of 1990, the Corporation reduced its assets by $4.3 billion and realized approximately $175 million in pre-tax sales. These sales were largely accomplished through the use of competitive auctions to ensure that the Corporation would maximize proceeds on sale. Assets are targeted to be reduced by a total of approximately $8 billion by year end, with additional pre-tax gains. See Note 1 on page 35 for further discussion of the asset disposition program.

The Corporation is dependent on continued asset sales to meet the immediate liquidity needs of its subsidiary banks and to reduce Federal Reserve discount window borrowings.

As of March 1990, the other affiliated banks, especially CBT, were providing a significant component of Bank of New England, N.A.'s liquidity through the provision of approximately $1.5 billion in daily federal funds. The ability of these banks to continue this funding is an important component of Bank of New England, N.A.'s present liquidity.

As mentioned earlier, in their eagerness to increase loans outstanding, lenders often overlook the financial dynamics of their customers. Another form of management effectiveness relates to how customers are managed by specialty-lending groups. Banks often establish industry groups for better market penetration but do not take into account the basic differences in financial requirements of the types of companies included in the group. In forming these groups, it is essential to form them with compatible financial dynamic characteristics in mind; the differences in operating leverage from one borrower to the next are often ignored.

Operating leverage involves the company's fixed costs in relation to the margin that can be earned from additional sales; financial leverage involves the impact on the balance sheet as a result of the financing methods chosen. Companies that depend upon the conversion of raw materials to finished goods are more dependent on fixed assets and have higher operating leverage than wholesalers; companies dependent upon the direct utilization of fixed assets to perform services (such as transportation companies) have higher operating leverage than those that perform services through use of labor. Since acceptable leverage is, in part, determined by reliability of earnings and cash flow, the amount of competition anticipated to be faced by a borrower is an important external factor. Therefore, government regulation of specific industries, whether by federal or by state commissions (FCC, ICC, etc.), allows companies in those industries to enjoy a monopolistic status, constricting competition but also making greater leverage more acceptable.

However, subsequent governmental elimination of the monopolistic status can have disastrous effects on both the companies themselves and on their lenders. The airline deregulation of the late 1970s is a case in point. Under prior regulation and control by the Civil Aeronautics Board, competition was restricted, and all fares had to be approved by the CAB. Because all airlines perform essentially identical services, they were awarded specific routes, some of which were profitable, offset by some that were marginal; and the general public was felt to be best served by government control of the system. The assured revenues allowed the airlines to finance the purchase of airplanes and facilities with far greater leverage than would have been acceptable without the monopolistic structure. Airlines provide transportation services, most of which are paid for very promptly, if not in cash, while the equipment used to provide the service is depreciated over several years. Individual airline revenues will vary due to seasonal travel patterns. In order to accommodate these fluctuations, a lot of aircraft financing was provided under "revolving lines of credit," allowing the airline to reduce its borrowings during the periods of cash surplus and yet to have funds available when revenues slowed during off seasons. The revolving credit was renewed every few years with the result that (as long as there were no defaults) only payments of interest were required, the only reduction in leverage coming from retained earnings. When the regulatory environment changed and the monopolistic structure was removed, however, competition increased incredibly on the most lucrative routes; the traditional route servers reduced rates, and other airlines entered those markets from which, under regulation, they had been excluded. The resulting reduction in fares and increase in number of flights reduced profitability to the point where the airlines with higher fixed costs for labor, facilities, and equipment—and the most debt—went into bankruptcy. Although deregulation could be said to be the primary cause of the widespread financial difficulty suffered by the established airlines at the time, failures since then reflect the inability to compete effectively in an open market, generally a result of bad management decisions in marketing, planning, and internal control.

In their eagerness to increase loans outstanding, lenders often overlook the financial dynamics of their customers, resulting in inappropriate loan structuring. Banks often establish industry groups for better market penetration but overlook the basic differences in financial dynamics of the companies included in the group. An excellent example of this was the formation by some of the larger banks of aerospace groups to finance the airlines and their suppliers, such as Boeing and Lockheed. The theory was that they would have a better chance at financing airlines if they could garner a reputation for financing the entire supply chain. However, the financial requirements of the aircraft buyer (engaged in providing transportation) and the aircraft manufacturer could not be more dissimilar. The marketing appeal was scant and the synergy almost nonexistent between the financing requirements of companies engaged in performing large, long-term government contracts as well as manufacturing commercial aircraft and their airline customers that provided a public transportation service. BNE did not have an aerospace group but did have a communications industry group that suffered from these and other, perhaps more insidious, problems. These problems are commented on in the relevant sections shown below from a memo to David Falwell, then the Credit Policy Officer.[10]

Bank of New England
Memorandum

To: David G. Falwell, Executive Vice President

From: Charles B.M. Douglas, Senior Vice President

Date: October 14, 1987

Re: LOAN CONTROL

I. General Discussion:

The function of Loan Control is that of both monitoring and maintaining the asset quality of the loan portfolio. This responsibility is centered in the BNE portfolio but it extends to those affiliates for which the Loan Review Department and Controlled Loan Department have been assigned overview responsibility. The responsibility for asset quality involves objective analysis of both the portfolio and the manner in which it is being administered, insuring that corporate goals for growth and profitability are not being attained at the expense of credit standards and that growth of group portfolios has not outstripped the abilities of the personnel who handle them.

The ability to *monitor* the asset quality of the portfolio is dependent upon the ability to evaluate the underlying credits on a continuing basis. This is accomplished by the quarterly group reviews of the BNE lower rated portfolio and by annual credit analysis by the Credit Department. This is augmented by annual profit center reviews performed by the Loan Review Department. These reviews not only cover the portfolio, but also review the credit administration procedures of the unit. While the system is adequate for those segments where growth has been relatively slow, it is inadequate for those areas where growth has been rapid and is further hampered by a shortage of qualified personnel. In some cases, sheer volume has rendered the process currently used to be largely ineffective. A new methodology is needed and will be developed during the next few months. The problem is presently evident in the three areas commented on below.

The ability to *maintain* asset quality is dependent upon the ability to effect change when and where it is appropriate. This area has always remained somewhat fuzzy in terms of execution, as the responsibility has been assigned but the authority has not. The result is that desired change has to be accomplished through departments which often have competing priorities.

Both the monitoring and maintenance of asset quality in the affiliated banks is advisory in nature in the same sense that a regular bank examination is advisory. The Controlled Loan aspects are more direct in that any loans in excess of $1 million which are designated either internally or by Loan Review are evaluated for handling by Controlled Loan in Boston and, at the option of BNE Boston may be taken over for handling.

II. Specific Areas Needing Attention:

A. Real Estate

Real estate credits are not based upon the same criteria as commercial credits. Failure of the Credit Department to address the issues properly resulted in analysis of all Real Estate proposals by Loan Review until '83 or '84, and a generally weak analytical specialty since. Most analyses are now essentially a restatement of the contact officer's memos outlining the proposal. In addition, the administration of the department was based heavily on group leader and contact officer knowledge of his customer and project. While legal documentation has generally been good, follow up on requirements by LAC and file maintenance has not been. This condition is aggravated by an imposed rating system which is both very cumbersome and inflexible. In the last 18–24 months we have expanded the loan portfolio by a multiple of 4 and reduced our credit standards materially to meet competition. It is safe to say that the quality of the portfolio is worse than it was, that it is *probably* still *okay*, but that we really don't know.

Required Action:

1. Tighten credit administration–follow up:

2. Adopt (develop) appropriate rating system:

3. Evaluate the portfolio against ratings:

4. Revise system for keeping ratings current.

B. Communications

The Communications Department is characterized by having a very dominant leadership which practices the player-coach management style. In this case, however, there would appear to be much more emphasis on the player aspects than on the coaching ones.

This group covers CATV, radio, TV broadcasting, paging companies and bill board companies. While these have a common characteristic, the transmission of information to a large public, their financial characteristics are different enough to make assuming too many similarities dangerous. Analysis of these companies focuses on cash flows rather than the more usual credit factors and the analytical work is handled by a limited number of trainees "specializing" in this area. The analysts depend upon the members of the Communication Group to provide them with industry trends, standards, characteristics and acceptable financing practice because there is no other ready source for the information. The trouble is that, other than for CATV, the group's members themselves are not really knowledgeable enough to be able to provide objective and appropriate information because of the recency of their own exposure to the segment of the industry addressed. The department, however, dominates the analysts and the analyses reflect it.

Because the statistical comparisons differ from "usual" credits special formats are needed to monitor progress against projections, variance from which can signal serious problems in debt service and collateral value. The Credit Department does not prepare these spreads on an interim (or for that matter, fiscal) basis and the Communications Department has not been able to find the time to develop an acceptable format for over four years. We have not had a really satisfactory review of the portfolio for the last couple of years and none at all for the last six months because the department head is the only one who can do it and she never has enough time to get ready. The nature of the portfolio is changing due to the addition of broadcasting, etc. and in addition is a multiple of what it was two years ago. As with the Real Estate portfolio, credit standards have become more lax with competition. While documentation is probably in good shape, follow up is clearly not judging from loans that have recently been transferred to Controlled Loan. The CATV portion is likely in good shape because the industry still has fairly stable characteristics, but the quality of the rest of the portfolio can only be assumed satisfactory. We really don't know.

Required Action:

1. Tighten credit administration–particularly follow-up;

2. Establish format for interim tracking;

3. Reestablish and maintain review schedule.

C. Community Banking Portfolio

The demands on Loan Review for examining lending group portfolios, affiliated banks, preparation of reports and the 5–6 reviews have left little or no time to develop a reasonable loan review program for loans under $500 thousand, which includes virtually all of the loans in Community Banking. Demands on Controlled Loan resulting from the addition of Patriot and the yet-to-be tackled assignment of loans > $1 million in the affiliates has not left time to come up with a solution to the work-out problems of loans < $250 thousand. The

> need for attention to this area of the portfolio is clearly evident within the BNE portfolio and more recently indications have been made by some of the affiliates that they want help below the $1 million level.
>
> Action Required:
>
> 1. Develop a program for BNE < $500 thousand reviews;
>
> 2. Develop a program for handling < $250 thousand work-out loans within BNE;
>
> 3. Develop a program for < $1 million work-out loans in affiliate portfolios. [Etc.]

As indicated in this memo, BNE fell prey to the temptation to overlook the financial dynamics of customers in favor of marketing efforts, often resulting in inappropriate loan structuring.

Arrogantly Protecting Weaker Large Borrowers

As pointed out in the memo, some of these problems had been apparent for some time, but no action had been taken by the Credit Policy Officer to correct them, nor had the authority to correct them been granted to either Loan Review or Loan Control. This inaction sent an implicit message that led the lending groups to prioritize marketing at the expense of sound administration. Wilson was president of the BNENA, Jim Sweeney was the head of the Real

Estate Department, and Falwell was the Credit Policy Officer. It was not unusual for them to try to persuade the Loan Review Department to upgrade unfavorable ratings, particularly on larger loans that had been adversely rated. Their attempts were not successful, but their attempts at rate improvement set a poor example and detracted from the professed need for appropriate rating by the lending staff. The risks resulting from a lack of attention to sound loan administration remained unaddressed.

Specialized lending groups tend to develop a somewhat arrogant attitude toward the rest of their institution—an attitude that implies that other employees simply do not understand the nature of these specialty industries. At BNE, this attitude masked an incomplete understanding of some of the basic risk factors by the specialty group members themselves. This was often evidenced by the use of words they perceived to be industry jargon, picked up from members of specialty lending groups in other lending institutions. An amusing incident occurred with the communications group when they had begun to solicit broadcasting business from radio station owners and station buyers. Members of the group would frequently refer to the "stick value" of a given station, and the term appeared in the analyses prepared by aspiring members of the Credit Department. It was explained to members of the Loan Approval Committee (in a somewhat condescending manner) that the *stick value* was a basic industry term that referred to the inherent value of a radio station derived from a combination of the broadcasting license, the power of the broadcasting equipment, and the nature of the market area that the station covered. In order to further educate the LAC members about the radio industry, the communications group leader called a special meeting of the LAC to meet with a recognized industry expert, a publisher of an industry magazine that was highly regarded within the industry for its wide coverage of industry affairs. At one point during the expert's presentation, an LAC member asked, "How reliable is the stick value of a radio station?" The expert paused and asked, "What do you mean by 'stick value'?" When the meaning of the term was explained to him, he answered that it was an interesting term, but not one he had heard before.

The expert went on to say that the license, as such, has no value because it is a right awarded by the FCC to a specific party or group of people to allow them to broadcast on a specific frequency in a given area. It cannot be purchased. It is awarded free by the FCC and is not transferable in the usual sense since the proposed new broadcaster must receive approval of the FCC. After completing its vetting process, the FCC awards a new license to the new party, and the right of the former station owner to broadcast on that frequency is withdrawn. The granting of a license to one broadcaster to broadcast on one frequency does not preclude the FCC from awarding licenses to other groups to broadcast on different frequencies within the same area. The expert then explained how the potential of an area is estimated based on the demographics within the area for which a license to use a specific frequency has been granted. All of this information was new to those attending the meeting, even though the communications group had been operating for well over a year. This story amply demonstrates the bank's tendency to obfuscate truly critical financial information with catchy industry phrases that belied their actual ignorance of the industry practices; they inflated the values to suit the requirements instead of objective analysis.

Failure to Monitor and Respond Appropriately to Actual Borrower Performance

The impact of existing competition and new entrants into any given market was often played down in discussions at the LAC, the emphasis having been put on the superior management and marketing expertise of the proposed borrower. An excerpt from the comments regarding one of the communications group borrowers appearing in the communications group annual review prepared in August 1988 by the Loan Review Department is enlightening:[11]

> Operating performance [of the borrower] has been disappointing due to the expansion into the Florida market and intense competition in the Cape Cod market compounded by a difficult management situation. 1987 marked the first year of operation in Florida under the new ownership and performance was impacted by staffing problems (high turnover) and technical weaknesses. Expenses increased significantly.

> A new management team has been engaged to effect a turnaround. Also, a new tower will be built to accommodate the increase in power, as approved by the FCC, to 50,000 WATTS. This will facilitate broader market coverage in a high growth area and should enhance station value. The Cape Cod station, which remains #1 in the market, has experienced a sharp drop in market share from 28% to 21% due to new competition (three new stations) and a weak local economy. A new general manager has been hired to stabilize the situation. Overall the company did not manage the transition to two stations effectively.
>
> Consolidated NOI for fiscal 1987 was $1.1MM compared to projections of $1.5MM. Total revenues were $3.5MM versus $3.8MM projected. First quarter 1988 performance reflects continued weakness with NOI of $161M on revenue $720M which was inadequate to cover interest expense of $230M.
>
> A rating change to #6 is warranted given the weak operating performance, competitive challenges, management changes, personnel problems, minimal owner equity, and need for new capital. While many of the concerns are being addressed, this relationship requires continued close following.

It was obvious that this company was not taking the steps that they should have taken and that it was failing. As the final paragraph clearly indicates, the communications group had deliberately ignored all the warning signs.

It is critical for management to correlate product characteristics with internal process controls, and in the case of commercial banks, the nature of certain types of loans (their characteristics) requires that internal processes include not only careful evaluation of the borrowers' managements and financial conditions before the loans are granted, but also the effective monitoring of the borrowers' performance after the loans have been made. As stated elsewhere in this book, authority and responsibility are inseparable. It is incumbent on the loan approval body (in whatever form it exists) to take the responsibility for loans it approves, which result in losses, and it is the responsibility of the account officers to monitor closely the loans assigned to them and to report to their managers when borrowers are not performing as well as projected at the time of loan approval. At the Bank of New England, the approval process for larger loans effectively absolved both the loan approval committees and the account officers of any responsibility for credit worthiness. In addition, management failed to assure that all loan management procedures were adequate. In some lending groups, loans, after being made, were effectively ignored rather than being closely monitored by account officers. When problems with a borrower were finally recognized, the loan had deteriorated to the workout stage and, in some cases, to the point of bankruptcy.

Credit Administration Policies

Information Systems Are Not Management

It is obvious that reliable information is essential for making intelligent, reasoned decisions. Information systems must be appropriate for the nature and size of the business being operated and are necessary for measuring the degree to which all of the required functions of management are being properly carried out. The use of the word *systems* should not be limited in definition to computerized or other mechanical reporting and recording systems but should include written reports and whatever automated procedures are appropriate and necessary. Standard operating procedures should specify how management will (1) ensure that the responsibility for all necessary functions is properly assigned, (2) measure the effectiveness with which those responsibilities are being discharged, (3) take appropriate action to address problems as they become known, and (4) judge whether the original assumptions as to credit worthiness remain valid. The evaluation of the effectiveness with which certain functions are carried out is often assisted by computer or mechanically generated reports. It is important to remember, however, that mechanical systems only provide information as part of the basis for making decisions; they cannot make management decisions. Unless the information gathered is utilized by management in an intelligent manner, the most efficient systems devised will not prevent a business failure. Too often, management is lulled into a false sense of security by the generation of reports simply because the equipment is capable of producing them. Far more useful than the volume and diversity of the reports is the relevance of the information, management's interpretation, and the resulting actions taken.

Focus Shifts Require Recalibration of Checks and Balances

Effective administration of any organization requires the maintenance of effective checks and balances. By definition, this requires that certain activities be balanced by others, and in banking, the credit-marketing activities of the institution must be balanced by independent judgment in administering credit. Credit administration begins with analysis of the loan proposals by the Credit Department, followed by the loan approval process, the booking of approved loans, and then the process of managing the portfolio once the loans are booked. Undue emphasis by senior management on increasing loan volume and the perceived increase in internal political power that comes with successful marketing can often result in an adversarial relationship between the credit administration function and the marketing side. If either side becomes dominant, the overall goal of the organization of sound, cohesive growth can become subverted. At one point in the late 1970s, for instance, the executive vice president in charge of commercial lending at Irving Trust Company sought to "keep our powder dry" by restricting marketing efforts so severely that there was practically no growth at all. On the other hand, the experience of the savings and loan industry and of some commercial banks during the 1980s shows the disaster that can result from overly aggressive marketing accompanied by inadequate credit administration and control. The major deficiencies at BNE resulted from a fatal combination of questionable credit standards, inadequate or unreliable information, and a failure to react properly to the information that was provided.

Quality, Credibility, and Morale Go Hand in Hand

The complacency with unreliable information and the absence of a system with adequate checks and balances undermined management credibility and employees' pride in quality performance. The following story illustrates the level of pride that had traditionally existed at BNE. During the 1950s, the Credit Department received all incoming credit inquiries. The procedure called for the management trainees to conduct all credit investigations and prepare answering letters for signature by the bank's senior lender, Charles C. Kimball, or in his absence, the next most senior officer on the platform. Some of the inquiries were from existing customers seeking information regarding extension of trade credit to their customers or prospects. One such account was the H. H. Brown Shoe Company who used our Credit Department extensively to determine the credit worthiness of retailers and others buying from them on normal or extended trade terms. I investigated a retailer on the West Coast for them, and in the letter written for Mr. Kimball's signature, I commented, among other things, that the subject of the credit investigation was a "small retail chain store engaged in the distribution of inexpensive men's, women's, and children's shoes." The letter was returned to me for revision with the comment that the store was engaged in the distribution of inexpensive shoes for men, women, and children. The insistence management placed on grammatical precision was symptomatic of the emphasis placed on the quality and accuracy with which it sought to conduct all of its affairs. The bank was small by today's standards, and while the conservative nature of banking at the time pretty much precluded first-name-basis relationships between the staff and the older officers, the employees had a strong feeling of pride and caring about the institution.

During the spring of 1987, the effects of the CBT merger were filtering down through the organization, and morale at Bank of New England was perceptibly low. Management had decided to centralize all computer operations in the name of greater efficiency. The goal may have been admirable, but the implementation was far from it. All areas of the bank were affected by the change. The impact on the customers, particularly those with long-term relationships with the affiliates outside of Boston, was felt almost immediately. Personnel with daily customer contact were overwhelmed with complaints about errors in their accounts, and they in turn complained to their superiors about the frequency of mistakes being made. Unfortunately, Loan Operations adopted the attitude that rather than being a support service for the lending and investment services the bank provided to the general public, the bank's most important function was data processing, and they showed little to no interest in the problems created by the implementation of the centralization. It got to the point where personnel at most levels had an acronym for the answers they got when trying to deal with the operations in Boston: DILLIGAS (pronounced *dilligas*), which stood for "Do I look like I give a shit?" As mentioned in the chapter entitled "Orphaned Portfolios," for some obscure reason, Loan Operations in Boston went so far as to refuse to provide copies of the notes and documents of the portfolios of the former Lawrence and Gloucester banks to Bank of New England, North and Bank of New England, Essex when the responsibilities for these loan portfolios were finally assigned to them. In many ways, it was a symptom of the breakdown in interdepartmental cooperation throughout the system.

In the aftermath of this centralization, management decided to invite all employees to complete a confidential survey in order to determine the areas of discontent as precisely as possible. Once completed, questionnaires were collected and redistributed back to each division. Each division was to summarize its own questionnaires and discuss the results with department managers to see what constructive steps could be taken in hopes of alleviating the causes of low morale. This piecemeal approach effectively discouraged identification and resolution of cross-departmental problems.

The credit administration division results were summarized by the Credit Department and their findings distributed to all of the division department managers for study. Responses to the questionnaires made it abundantly clear that a major issue was the feeling that the quality of our services and reports was suffering materially and that nobody seemed to care. People were discouraged by their lack of confidence in the work of their fellow employees and by the apparent absence of concern by bank leadership. When the managers' meeting was held to discuss the report, I commented that, in view of the fact that concern about declining quality appeared to be a major issue, it was interesting to note that the survey summary report contained at least one major grammatical or typographical error on every single page. Nobody had proofread the report—not the typist, not her superior, not the department head. The head of the Credit Department, whose responsibility it had been to produce the report, began to stammer about insufficient time and a heavy workload. Ignoring his remarks, the division manager simply said, "Stop concentrating on the negative, for Christ's sake! Let's focus on the issues!" The manager didn't understand that his tacit acceptance of shoddy work—in a business that relies on attention to detail—overlooked a warning about the lack of concern for quality performance.

Cross-Functional Goals and Accountability for Their Attainment

Indifference to quality standards and performance often spreads from one group to another, particularly when the managers of interdependent groups cannot agree on synergistic priorities. Differences can arise between loan operations and lending groups and administrative groups, for example, where disagreement on procedures and forms can escalate into more serious problems. Unless the issues are addressed intelligently and promptly at higher levels, the groups tend to become more polarized and less flexible in adapting to each other's needs; communication deteriorates, frustrations mount, and efficiency suffers. This prolonged conflict is caused by the failure of management to make sure that the goals and priorities of the different areas of the bank are not in conflict with the attainment of overall corporate goals and priorities. Failure to hold department heads accountable for interdepartmental cooperation ultimately results in loss of respect for management and in marked reduction in the quality of job performance.

This had occurred at the Bank of New England. In order to avoid confrontation, consensus between groups was demanded where polarization had already precluded it. Problems between interoperational groups went unresolved, and the quality of performance for the institution as a whole declined steadily. Senior management decisiveness and leadership were absent when they were most needed.

In order to be effective, an organization should have at least one goal that is shared by a majority of its members—that is, a superordinate goal. Due to the diversity of functions and responsibilities, quality of performance is one common goal in most successful organizations. The quality of and pride in the work produced by an organization, either for outside or internal consumption, are good indicators of the quality of its leadership. I am reminded of an incident that occurred while I was office head of Irving Trust Company's 245 Park Avenue office in New York. One of our good customers was the Norman Morris Company, which had the sole distributorship of Omega watches in the United States. I had invited Mr. Morris (president and CEO), his son Robert, and his son-in-law also named Robert for luncheon in our 245 Park Avenue dining room. I had spoken to Mr. Morris about an Omega watch we had given one of our sons upon his going away to college. Our son played lacrosse, often playing with his watch on, resulting in its having been damaged with a lacrosse stick. During the lunch, I took the watch out and gave it to Mr. Morris, who said, "We'll take care of it" and passed it on to his son, Robert, who, in turn, handed it to his brother-in-law. The brother-in-law took one look at it and exclaimed with surprising anger and emotion, "This watch has been abused!" His obvious pride in their products extended to caring about them even after they had been sold. Their company was one of the most successful quality watch distributors in the country, in no small measure because they cared.

The degree to which inefficiency and carelessness are tolerated is an indicator of management concern for quality. Employees who are not bothered by careless mistakes lack the discipline and motivation to perform well, and if management is blind to the attitude of its employees or does little or nothing to correct it, the discipline and quality of the entire organization ultimately will suffer.

There is a story about an Arab on a journey. He had trekked across the desert all day and, finally tired and hot, decided to pitch his camp for the night. He put up his tent, put down his rugs, and lit his lamp. He sat down and pulled out a bowl of dates for his dinner. He picked up the first date and, by the light of the lamp, saw that it had a worm in it. He put the date aside and took out another date. He saw that it too had a worm in it, so he put it aside and took a third date from the bowl. The third date also had a worm in it, so he blew out the lamp and ate the rest of the dates in the bowl. The Arab might not have liked the idea of eating wormy dates, but he was hungry and knew that they were not toxic. On the other hand, when BNE decided to blow out the candle on accepted credit policies and traditional standards out of a hunger for growth, they improperly assessed the risk, and that decision turned out to be fatal.

Valuing "Belonging" Over Objectivity

At BNE, the Credit Policy Officer (CPO) was responsible for the credit administration division. The division was responsible for the maintenance of quality in the loan portfolio by ensuring that all necessary policies and procedures were effectively in place and by taking appropriate action to correct deficiencies as they were uncovered. Division management was ineffective in discharging these responsibilities. The deterioration of quality of the loan portfolio did not stem from a lack of analytical skills on the part of credit administration personnel, but rather from a conscious subordination of analytical insight by the Credit Policy Officer and some of his subordinates in an attempt to be seen as "belonging" in the marketing camp and to be perceived as positive, creative "members of the team." The objectivity required for true checking and balancing was all but abandoned for fear of offending lending group managers and account officers. The consequences were severe, ultimately contributing to the failure of the institution. Management deficiencies included the following:

- Tacit complicity in the erosion of credit standards
- Failure to insist on the development and maintenance of departmental staffing levels
- Failure to supervise and enforce the establishment of procedures necessary for sound loan management within lending groups

- Acceptance of novel types of financing with enthusiasm but no real understanding of inherent risks
- Failure to develop proper guidelines
- Misguided application of proven lending principles appropriate for one industry to another where they simply did not apply

There are copies of memos dating back to at least 1982 that chronicle the decline in credit standards in the real estate and specialty lending groups at Bank of New England. Examples of misapplied principles follow in the next chapter. They are not isolated instances but rather are illustrative of the misguided approach to credit administration. In addition, as stated elsewhere, promotions were often made on an emotional basis rather than on a rational, objective analysis of the individuals' ability to carry out the responsibilities of the positions being filled. Aggravating the situation, there was an unhealthy jealousy between Bank of New England, NA and Connecticut Bank and Trust, each vying for the "leadership" position. BNENA appeared loathe to admit to any deficiency in credit skills by bringing in an outsider to fill the position of head of real estate lending or any other major position. Accordingly, James Sweeney, then Senior Vice President in the Real Estate Department, was favored as head of real estate lending by Richard Driscoll, and recommendations to look outside the bank for a group leader were ignored.

Sacrificing Standards for Fast Growth

BNE started real estate construction lending in a small way in the late 1950s with unsecured loans to well-known, well-capitalized developers such as Cabot, Cabot & Forbes. It gradually expanded into making construction loans to less well-capitalized firms, then requiring that contractors be covered by construction bonds and that developers be bonded and have firm takeouts for completed projects. As building in the United States continued to grow in the late 1960s and early 1970s, banks in general began lending to real estate investment trusts (REITs). Bank of New England, no exception, added participations with other larger banks to its portfolio. It was also active in the local markets with local developers. When the real estate markets softened and the REIT craze subsided, BNE took its losses and workouts and pulled back in the market.

During the next several years, BNE policy was to go back to lending 75% against construction costs, and the developer had to have completion bonds and a firm takeout from an acceptable source. Generally speaking, the loans were made to single-project developers to build one project at a time. When the market began to expand again in 1983–1984, BNE naturally wanted to participate in its growth. The bank responded to growing demand for aggressive lending by progressively eroding its credit standards. With the looming expiration of certain tax benefits for new projects, the pressure grew to get as many loans as possible approved by the end of 1986. The volume of loan requests after December 1986 initially dropped off as expected, but the ready availability of financing soon offset the expired tax benefits, and the volume of new projects soon exceeded the pre-1987 levels. A new demand developed to finance one project at a time for developers with multiple, but a limited number, of projects. Due to their project-by-project financing background, both the Real Estate Department and the analysts in the Credit Department downplayed the risk that the developer might use the funds drawn for one project on another. This persisted despite the risks inherent in that practice being pointed out by Loan Review. Analysts routinely confined their analyses to single projects rather than considering the developer's consolidated cash flow and requirements. Soon the pressure grew to advance up to 80% of project costs and then to forego the requirement for a firm takeout, provided that the developer had a signed lease on the project from an acceptable lessee when completed. If the project were a mall, a lease with an acceptable anchor tenant was required. The theory was that the risk was reduced to that of having the developer complete the project as, when complete, the lessee would occupy the building (or in the case of a mall with a good anchor tenant, the balance of the space would quickly lease up), and a takeout could be readily accomplished. The erosion continued, however, first going to 100% financing of project costs and then to the elimination of lease-up requirements, the argument being that the elimination of a requirement of preleasing would give the developer more leverage in dealing with potential lessees.

Encouraging Marginal Loans from Field Affiliates

In 1987, the president of BNENA was promoted to chairman, and his successor as president, the former head of commercial banking division, also became the chairman of the Senior Loan Approval Committee. Loan Control hoped that the credit standards would be tightened as the new chairman had had extensive experience as a commercial lender. One of the first credits presented for approval was that of a deal proposed by the Bank of New England affiliate in Lowell. The loan was too large for their local approval, so it had been referred to Boston. It called for a loan to finance construction of a condominium building in Nashua, New Hampshire. The site was nearly surrounded by a river, railroad tracks, and some old, disused mill buildings. The sole access to the property was a narrow road cutting between two of the unoccupied mill buildings and across the railroad tracks, clearly not an attractive proposition. Very tight financial support and an oversupply of condominiums in the Nashua market completed the list of shortcomings, all of which were quite clearly pointed out in the analysis. Nonetheless, the new SLAC chairman approved the loan with the comment that we had to "encourage our affiliated bank officers," presumably reasoning that his show of eagerness to support the officers "in the field" would encourage them to bring in more proposals. However, it only encouraged those in the field to solicit loans from borrowers who could not find other financing. As one real estate officer remarked after the bank had failed, “They [the bank] seemed to want the marginal crap, so that’s what we gave them.”

Deep—but Empty—Pockets

Shortly after the Nashua loan request, we received a proposal from the Philadelphia Loan Production Office to finance the purchase of a building in Princeton, New Jersey, by a local investor. Although the building was fairly new and in a good location, it was let to IBM on a long-term lease. Capitalized at the rate of return in the lease and compared to current interest rates, the building was then worth about $16 million. The investor felt strongly that the interest rates were going to drop, and the building, given the lower interest rates, would then be worth $20 million, which he was willing to pay for it. He intended to put down $4 million and borrow the remaining $16 million. The investor was said to have “deep pockets” in the event that more cash was needed to support debt service. The analysis pointed out that the market value of the building was $16 million, and we were lending 100% of the market value; the comment was made by Loan Control that we wouldn’t lend 100% of the market value of government bonds, let alone a piece of real estate. It was also financing nothing short of an interest rate speculation. The chairman approved the loan on the basis that the $4 million was 20% of the purchase price. Any hopes for tighter credit standards evaporated completely. As it turned out, interest rates did not take the turn the investor expected, his "deep pockets" were not deep enough, and the loan was ultimately transferred to the Controlled Loan Department.

Hasty Assessment of the Tip of the Iceberg

As an aside, it is interesting to note that unraveling of the real estate portfolio was exposed two years later with the regulators' criticism of the Bank of New England, North (Lowell) real estate business. As mentioned earlier, the projected losses made the local newspapers, and in April 1989, both the chairman of Bank of New England Corporation (Walter Connolly) and the chairman of Bank of New England, NA (Richard Driscoll) were quoted in the *Boston Globe* blaming the management of Bank of New England, North and their lack of sound lending policies. They stated that, in retrospect, the pressure to acquire new banks as a result of the change in interstate banking regulations perhaps had resulted in a hasty assessment of the management of some of the banks being acquired, weaknesses in management that did not appear until the real estate market in northern Massachusetts and southern New Hampshire began to soften. In fact, Bank of New England, North was then the relatively recent result of combined operations with other affiliated banks, and a great many of their problems stemmed from the transfer to them of the portfolios of the Cape Ann National Bank in Gloucester and the Bay State Merchants National Bank of Lawrence. These accounts had been badly neglected by Bank of New England, Boston when the management of those institutions left, and responsibility for them was transferred to the Boston bank. In addition, the banks that were combined to form Bank of New England, North had been owned by Bank of New England Corp. for at least three years or longer, ample time to assess the quality and capability of their management.

After having encouraged affiliated banks' officers by approving questionable loans for them in the Boston bank and by transferring the Cape Ann and Lawrence portfolios to them after a prolonged period of near abandonment, the incident brought to mind the sign in a home workshop that read simply, "I am fairly intelligent myself, but I have a lot of stupid help." As it turned out, Bank of New England, North was merely the tip of the Boston bank's real estate and communications iceberg—the iceberg that ultimately caused the bank's failure. Following is an excerpt from the 10-K filed for Bank of New England as of December 31, 1989:[12]

> The Corporation during 1989 experienced a significant increase in the level of nonperforming assets and charge-offs. The allowance for possible credit losses increased from $325 million at the beginning of the year to $1.521 billion by December 31, 1989, and the provision for possible credit losses increased from $123 million in 1988 to $1.614 billion in 1989. Fourth quarter examination of the credit portfolio by the OCC and the Corporation led to a large number of charge-offs and downgrades in risk ratings in the loan portfolio, which led to the provision taken during the fourth quarter of 1989.

> As a result, the Corporation recorded a $1.11 billion loss in 1989. The 1989 loss, coupled with deteriorating asset quality, has had a substantial adverse effect on the Corporation's capital, liquidity, and earnings. Equity capital was 1.54% of assets as of December 31, 1989, compared to 5.10% December 31, 1988. Since the December 15, 1989 preliminary announcement of the projected loss, a deposit and funding outflow of over $7 billion has occurred. In late January, due to these deposit withdrawals, the Corporation began borrowing from the Federal Reserve Bank's discount window. Although the level of borrowings changes from day to day, and has been as high as $2.3 billion, on March 28, 1990 the federal borrowing balance was $1.7 billion. The Corporation has deposited with the Federal Reserve Bank of Boston approximately $15 billion of collateral, primarily loans of the Bank of New England banks, for these borrowings. This collateral provides a maximum of approximately $8 billion of borrowing potential at the window, although there is no assurance that the Fed would advance the maximum amount. The Corporation's debt issues have been downgraded to below investment grade, and the Corporation has stopped issuing commercial paper.

The efforts of the affiliated banks to keep the Bank of New England from failing proved unsuccessful, and the Bank of New England ultimately dragged the balance of the corporation into liquidation.

Frequent Approvals "Out of Committee"

Just as the rising tide floats all ships, the growth in the real estate market, combined with the length of time it took for project-related problems to surface, had fueled more aggressive lending practices. The Real Estate Department and the analysts in the Credit Department developed a euphoric approach to lending. The chairman of the Senior Loan Approval Committee continued to approve virtually anything that was presented, and loans approved out of committee (LAOCs) continued to constitute a significant percentage of all large loans approved. LAOCs, by definition, were those approved by the chairman of the committee without presentation to the full committee and were done on the premise that time constraints prevented the full analysis normally required by the committee. In spite of the increasing risk

"Most people would jump at an opportunity like this."

and complexity of both real estate and communications industry lending activities, Credit Administration continued to "cooperate," thereby abrogating their responsibilities for appropriate guidelines and proper loan management in departments where it was obviously lacking. In short, no discipline was exerted over the geographical locations in which loans were sought, the quality of the loans being made, or the manner in which they were managed by the various lending groups. The volume of out-of-market loans generated by the Philadelphia office grew rapidly, and projects in areas of the country where the bank had no experience were readily approved. They included, for example, a $25 million loan to construct a discount center in a small town off a main highway in South Carolina, the "equity" for the project being a $5 million second mortgage on a mall in Georgia, that mall being subject to a $25 million first mortgage and an estimated market value of $30 million. The fact that the assumed $5 million equity was already supporting a $25 million loan and the inaccessibility of that equity were not considered detrimental. Since the bank was not familiar with the area or the borrower, sound credit principles would have dictated that the requirements for acceptance be far more stringent (rather than less stringent) than would have been the case with a known borrower in a familiar territory.

These loans were often accompanied by limited rather than full guarantees, the exposure of the guarantors often limited to their investments in numbers of limited partnerships, many of undetermined financial strength. The increasing loan volume paradoxically seemed to generate more confidence in the lending staff rather than raising concerns about the quality of loan standards and departmental loan management. It is reminiscent of the story about the eternal optimist who fell off a building and, as he plunged past the thirtieth floor, said to a person in the window, "I'm all right so far!" As mentioned above, real estate loans that would not have been considered in 1986 were almost routinely approved in 1987 either by the Senior Loan Approval Committee or the SLAC chairman out of committee, regardless of apparent risk. Three examples of this follow; two relate to real estate and the third to a leveraged buy-out financing.

The first was a $32 million loan with a limited guarantee of $4 million to two Boston real estate developers to allow them to purchase and upgrade a 95%-occupied apartment complex in Phoenix, Arizona. The developers' idea did not succeed in practice. When the upgrades took place and the rents were increased, the tenants left. The guarantors gave the bank $4 million (representing the amount of their guarantee) and turned the project over to the bank, leaving a balance of $28 million. When the loan was turned over to the Controlled Loan Department, the newly assigned officer went to Phoenix, researched population changes and growth, and discovered that there was a four-year supply overhang of equivalent quality apartments in the area. Capitalized at reasonable occupancy rates, the project was worth only about $16 million. At that time, the Controlled Loan Department was recommending a charge-off of $8 million. Walter Connolly attended the meeting, and on hearing the recommendation, he looked down the length of the table to Driscoll and asked, "Why did we make this loan? How could we do this?" Driscoll responded, "Well, it seemed like a good idea at the time." Six months after the loan was made, the bank charged off an additional $4 million.

A second example is a loan that was made to a large developer in the Boston area, A. J. Lane, who was having severe financial problems and was being threatened with bankruptcy by unpaid creditors and with foreclosures by mortgage lenders. They had approached the head of the Real Estate Department for a loan of sufficient size to mollify the unsecured creditors and forestall any foreclosure actions. In return, they would finance all their future projects through Bank of New England.

The amount of the loan was about $25 million. Some members of the Senior Loan Approval Committee raised serious doubts, suggesting that if the loan were to be made at all, A. J. Lane should file for Chapter 11 Bankruptcy, and the bank could participate in financing the reorganization; one even suggested that the loan should be made and handled in the Controlled Loan Department since it was a workout to begin with. Nonetheless, the decision was made to approve and handle it as a routine loan, and in effect, the Real Estate Department joined the Commercial Finance Department in apparent willingness to be a "lender of last resort" (see the response to the October 26, 1982, memo to the Credit Policy Officer). A. J. Lane remained out of bankruptcy for a short period and then filed for protection under Chapter 11 of the Bankruptcy Code. The loan was subsequently transferred to the Controlled Loan Department for handling. The A.J. Lane loss, as one would expect given the conditions under which it was made, was very substantial. The head of Loan Control was later approached by an irate director of a small local savings bank. The savings bank had wanted to begin lending in commercial real estate and, because of the excellent reputation that Bank of New England had built over the years, asked if they could participate in one of the BNE loans. The Real Estate Department gave them a $3 million participation in the loan to A. J. Lane, on which they shortly suffered a total loss.

A third example was a proposal originated by the loan representative in Chicago, a young woman hired from another bank to assist in finding leveraged buy-out opportunities. She had heard that another group of banks apparently was balking at increasing to $140 million the amount of their outstanding loan to Graybill, a company started by a welder named Stoecker. Stoecker's rise had begun with the purchase, rehabbing and selling of some run-down Chicago real estate, after which he had purchased several small operations, successfully tapping into the LBO marketing efforts of the banking industry. Walter Connolly, chairman of Bank of New England Corp., was sufficiently intrigued to fly out to Chicago to meet with the bank representative and the proposed borrower. Based upon his request, Connecticut Bank & Trust approved both a $70 million participation in the $140 million request and its own service as the agent for the entire credit and asked Bank of New England, NA to take $30 million of CBT's $70 million. The head of the BNENA's national accounts division in Boston presented the proposal at CBT's request but was not at all enthusiastic about it. When the borrower's background and experience were addressed and it was clearly pointed out that the big-eight accounting firm that had prepared the financial statements had refused to give an unqualified opinion on the borrower's financial condition, the full Senior Loan Approval Committee in Boston turned the loan down. Nonetheless, BNENA reversed itself, and the $30 million participation was approved "out of committee." Within months, Stoecker's problems surfaced, and Graybill filed for Chapter 11. The combined loss, commented upon by incredulous local newspapers, was one of the largest single losses in the bank's history.

As these three examples clearly illustrate, the deliberate overlooking of apparent risk had deeply eroded normal banking risk assessment. These were incredible risks taken for the sake of increasing loan volume.

Investment in a New and Volatile Industry

At Bank of New England, the communications group was formed in the early 1980s to capitalize on the exposure to the cable TV industry. The commercial banking division manager and one of his section managers had exposure to the industry; the division manager had worked for a CATV company, and the section manager had prior experience working for a bank that had loans to companies in the CATV industry. They, in turn, hired account officers from other banks with whom they were familiar to assist in the division's marketing efforts. The group covered CATV, radio, TV broadcasting, paging companies, and billboard companies.

The CATV industry was in transition, gaining some start-ups and undergoing consolidation with frequent mergers and acquisitions. The instability of the CATV industry should have been regarded as an additional risk factor. The new communications group regarded it as great marketing opportunity as acquisitions typically were financed with debt rather than equity. At the time there were aspects of the industry that were somewhat similar to those of regulated utilities (installed poles, lines, and cables, municipal restrictions on competition, etc.), but CATV companies clearly presented a greater risk. Based on public utility–financing principles, most of the division's early financing was based upon relatively conservative multiples of the historical cash flow. As the industry grew and consolidation heated up, however, the presumed logic of the division's risks became increasingly specious. The history of the cash flow of the acquiring companies frequently was very short. The multiples of projected cash flow became based upon the anticipated cash flow resulting from improved operations of the acquired companies (the underlying assumption being that the owners of the acquiring companies had superior expertise that would enable them to reach the "real" market potential). It was projected that the resulting "synergy" of the combined operations would improve the cash flow, so the division raised the multiples from seven or eight times combined actual cash flow to twelve to fifteen times anticipated, improved cash flow. The account officers and the division manager rationalized that the increased multiples were "traditional" practice. The division's financing of start-ups by experienced operators or entrepreneurial "recognized industry experts" were frequently supported by what was termed "sweat equity" (i.e., the principals' personal research and effort was considered the equivalent of a capital investment and sufficient equity behind the loan). Since the principals invested no cash, the bank provided it all, working capital as well as the acquisition financing.

Marketing Distracting from Performance Review

Although the bank as a whole had relatively limited exposure to the CATV industry, the guidelines for defining acceptable risk levels were established by the communications group itself, hell-bent on avoiding the possibility of an independent, well-researched study performed by the credit administration division that might have bridled their unbounded optimism. The head of the Senior Loan Approval Committee, who originally formed the communications group, agreed with the enthusiastic assumptions of the account officers and their division head, virtually assuring approval of their proposals. Once the loans had been booked, nearly the only measure of performance was a comparison of the company's actual customer and revenue growth against the projected growth included in the original credit analysis. The borrowers were to submit the information, and the tracking was to be performed by the account officers. In due course, the account officers became so engrossed in their marketing efforts that their monitoring of borrowers' compliance became lax, and their tracking of performance against projections became erratic. The Loan Review Department's ninety-day reviews began in a timely manner, but within a year the lack of information precluded meaningful oversight. The division head made repeated promises to take corrective action, but improvement was at best sporadic and happened, even then, only after the original commercial banking division manager, who by then was the president of the bank, was informed of the lack of ability to review the portfolio because of lax management.

The number of new loan requests slowed with the communications group's market penetration and the ongoing consolidation of the CATV industry. Marketing attention broadened to include other forms of media communication, such as television and radio broadcasting, movie theaters, and paging systems. The concept of lending on the assured cash flow generated by a public utility expanded first to include CATV and then to all media types. The same pattern of "traditional" cash flow multiples was adopted as the "industry standard," disregarding the volatility inherent in derivation of revenues from uncommitted sources, such as advertising, as opposed to revenue from CATV systems' viewers who were wired into the systems. What had started out as a truly traditional concept for the extension of credit was stretched beyond the point of reasonable risk.

Absence of Financial Covenants

Loan agreements typically include financial covenants to define the limits beyond which adverse changes in financial condition represent unacceptable risk, presumably giving the lending institution adequate warning for appropriate review and action. Proposed changes in protective covenants in the loan agreements, by policy, should have received the approval of the Loan Review Department. This did not happen. There was no enforcement of covenant modification procedures, as is pointed out in the communications group annual portfolio review dated August 31, 1988:[13]

> Unapproved Term Loans
>
> BNE's loan policy (CLM 12.41) requires Loan Review's approval on most term loans in excess of $250,000. The June 30, 1988 Unapproved Term Loan List generated by Credit Operations indicated 59 loans originated by the communications group in which covenants were not approved by Loan Review. This

> represents 36 obligors with total outstanding of more than $400 million. Reportedly, the high number of loans which are not reviewed through appropriate channels is caused by industry pressures and the complexities of each deal which necessitate constant negotiation, often right up to, or through, the closing date. Because of the time constraints and frequent changes, it is often impractical to keep Loan Review involved in the covenant approval process. This area of policy compliance requires review by the new Term Loan Administrator and the communications group Leader in order to develop procedures which will allow the necessary flexibility as well as substantive compliance with bank policy.

The reason reported above was really a lame excuse, the "industry pressure" in reality having been brought about by attempts to comply with borrower requests to waive the violations or to modify the covenants. Common sense would dictate that the greater the complexity of the deal, the greater its inherent risk and the greater the need for careful risk assessment, rather than a very willing compliance to change the rules. Some of these transactions were large enough and complex enough to warrant very careful and detailed analysis of covenant changes by the Loan Review Department, as required by policy, rather than being left to the discretion of the account officers and the group leader, who were preoccupied with loan growth at the expense of administrative detail. The loan cited below involved a total of $68 million agented by

BNENA, $65 million of which was participated in by other banks. This case (taken from the Communications Loan Review) also cites the failure of the borrower to provide the required financial information when results of operations clearly indicated the existence of severe problems.[14]

> FY 87 was an extremely disappointing one for *[the borrower]*. Ineffective management at several of the acquired stations, lack of attention to two of the weaker stations and the time spent putting together the Blair acquisition and subsequent resales led to disappointing revenue and cash flow, which fell well below budget.

	Budget (000's)	Actual	Actual
	FYE 12/31/86	FYE 12/31/86	FYE 12/31/87
Revenue	$33,629,763	$33,752,397	$39,040,245
NOI	4,065,572	8,525,525	4,209,911
SD/CF	16.96	7.98	NA
TD/CF	22.62	11.5	NA
CF/Debt Service	.43	.90	NA

> These results were in violation of all covenants. The covenants are in the process of being waived. Audited FYE 12/31/87 statements have yet to be issued because of the lack of a formal waiver of these covenants; approval of the waiver by the bank group was held up pending the completion

> of specific remedies which were required of [*the borrower*], as detailed below.
>
> 3) Concise monthly management reports are now compiled by *[the borrower]* and sent to BNE. This is in response to BNE's concern for not being kept abreast of 1987 results as they unfolded; reportedly, *[the borrower]* was aware of how poor the FYE results would be early as August/September, but did not communicate their revised projections to the Bank.

The high multiples of cash flow paid for acquisitions of all types of media companies were supported only by the willingness of banks to lend. When the regulators began criticizing what they termed highly leveraged transactions, the lending appetite was curbed, and the valuations and salability of CATV systems dropped dramatically. Many institutions suffered heavy losses as a result. The entire cycle, from start to finish, did not last long enough to establish anything remotely resembling true traditional practice.

Honest Analysis Experienced as a Barrier to Entry

Credit analysis is part of the trainees' preparation for commercial banking—standard practice in most commercial banks. However, the system of selecting credits for analysis inherently compromised everyone's objectivity. BNE analyst trainees were allowed to choose their own cases, and naturally, they tended to select credits in the lending area they wanted to join upon completion of their training. This would give them exposure to the industry and to the officers in the lending group. An analyst who prepared an objective analysis pointing out higher risk than the lending officer and department head wanted to acknowledge often found himself or herself unable to join the desired lending group when the training was complete. As pointed out below in the paragraphs of the October 14, 1987, memo addressed to David Falwell, then Credit Policy Officer, the objectivity of the Credit Department had become badly compromised.[15]

> Real estate credits are not based upon the same criteria as commercial credits. Failure of the Credit Department to address the issues properly resulted in analysis of all Real Estate proposals by Loan Review until '83 or '84, and a generally weak analytical specialty since. Most analyses are now essentially a restatement of the contact officer's memos outlining the proposal.
>
> The Communications Department is characterized by having a very dominant leadership which practices the player-coach management style. In this case, however, there would appear to be much more emphasis on the player aspects than on the coaching ones.
>
> The group covers CATV, radio, TV broadcasting, paging companies and bill board companies. While these have a common characteristic, the transmission of information to a large public, their financial characteristics are different enough to make assuming too many similarities dangerous. Analysis of these companies focuses

> on cash flows rather than the more usual credit factors and the analytical work is handled by a limited number of trainees "specializing" is this area. The analysts depend upon the members of the Communication Group to provide them with industry trends, standards, characteristics and acceptable financing practice because there is no other ready source for the information. The trouble is that, other than for CATV, the group's members themselves are not really knowledgeable enough to be able to provide objective and appropriate information because of the recency of their own exposure to the segment of the industry addressed. The department, however, dominates the analysts and the analyses reflect it.

The lending groups in general had apparently abandoned the concept that the Credit Department function is that of providing objective analysis of loan proposals rather than a reiteration of the lending officer's desires. Insisting on justification of loan proposals for consideration of future career paths was entirely inappropriate.

Spreading Problems in the Credit Department

These developments were attributable to a lack of objective oversight of the Credit Department by the Credit Administration Division staff member specifically responsible for it. Another example of the effects of bending standard procedures to please the loan-originating groups is illustrated below. Under generally accepted accounting principles, inventory on the balance sheet is to be carried at the lower of cost or market. The LIFO/FIFO issue relates to the valuation of those units remaining in inventory at the end of the year. Under the LIFO (last in, first out) basis of accounting, the items that were sold during the year are deemed to have been the last ones bought, and the cost of goods sold is charged accordingly. This is a sound approach, particularly in a period of rising prices, for it indicates whether or not a distributor, for example, is able to sell goods at a markup over replacement cost. If the distributor is unable to sell goods at a markup over replacement cost, it will be losing money on every sale and ultimately will fail. The result is that the items that were on hand at the beginning of the year are deemed to be the same items on hand at the end of the year and are carried at the same value as they were the prior year (i.e., the last items purchased for resale during the year are deemed to have been the first ones sold). This has tax implications in that the taxpayer is not forced to pay taxes on the increased value of his inventory resulting from inflation, and most companies use this method of accounting for submission of their tax returns and for submission to their banks. The FIFO (first in, first out) method of accounting for inventory values in financial statements, on the other hand, has not been used to any extent for many years because in times of rising prices, it can result in reporting inflated earnings and increased taxes and masks the borrower's markup on goods currently sold.

The special industries lending group had hired an aggressive young account officer to generate business in

Connecticut. He was good at bringing in proposals but had very weak credit skills, and most of the proposals he generated were from marginal companies, such as borrowers in the energy field whose current financial statements reflected unprofitable operations on a LIFO basis due to the rise in energy costs. Many others had operated at a loss due to changes in the cost of distributed or manufactured goods, increases they were unable to pass on to their customers. Credit administration yielded to pressure by the special industries group leader by switching to FIFO so as to reflect a "more accurate picture" and a more positive response to their marketing efforts. It brought to mind an incident that had happened in the late fifties regarding the submission of financial statements by automobile dealers financing their inventories on floor plans with the bank. The head of the consumer finance group making the loans educated us all one day by stating clearly that automobile dealers prepared three sets of financial statements: one for the IRS, one for the automobile manufacturers, and one for the bank. Obviously, he claimed, the bank got the accurate statements. After heavy losses, the bank got out of floor plan financing.

The use of FIFO ultimately proved unworkable because the required information often was not available, and the conversion of the statements from one format to another was cumbersome; it also resulted in an indefinite delay in getting the department to spread financial statements on the automated spread format requested by Loan Review to help them more readily identify borrower weaknesses. This was commented upon in the memo dated July 19, 1985, to Hugh Taylor, then Credit Policy Officer, which follows.[16]

Bank of New England
Memorandum

To: Hugh M. Taylor, Executive Vice President

From: Charles B. M. Douglas, Senior Vice President

Re: Controls

Date: July 19, 1985

The primary responsibility of the Loan Review Department is obviously that of a continual review of the quality of the loans in the portfolio. In the past, one of the most important segments of the review process consisted of a discussion between group leaders and division heads and the OIC Loan Review and OIC Loan Control. Initially, minutes as such were not kept formally. The information reviewed tended to be stale, with reviews consisting more of information presented by the group leader rather than a discussion with Loan Review. Growth of the portfolio required a change, as the total loan portfolio in 1976 to $472,000,000, and by 1982 it amounted to $1,600,000,000. In 1982 we began preparing and circulating formal minutes to insure that recommendations and plans of action developed at the review meetings would be followed up on by the group leaders, the reports of CFD examiners were reviewed prior to the meetings by Loan Review and more current financial information prepared by the Credit Department was evaluated.

As of June 30, 1985, the portfolio totaled $2,800,000,000. The loan review system clearly must have modifications to it if it is to continue to be effective because the volume of loans is such that there is simply not enough time available to become familiar enough with credits being reviewed to ask more than obvious questions. In addition, a great deal of the meeting time is taken by either repeating information that was available before or by focusing almost as much on those credits doing well as those whose trends are becoming adverse.

We had hoped that with automation of the Credit Department a report by profit center such as the one attached would be available prior to each profit center loan review. This would enable the review to focus on those credits needing attention and help detect adverse trends within the entire portfolio on a periodic basis. It is an important portfolio management tool. At my request a software program for doing this was completed by Pete Haynsworth from Credit and a data base loaded into it by Eileen Coombes from Loan Control in late 1984, the intent of having it in full use during, spreading it to the affiliates for better portfolio control purposes. While the program for producing this information is available, the input for it has essentially stopped, as the input is generated by the automated spread process in the Credit Department. No progress has been made for two reasons. The first delay lasted approximately six months and originated with an attempt by the Credit Department to present financial information prepared on a LIFO basis on a FIFO spread, which resulted in not spreading any LIFO financial statements on the automated

CDO0023

Hugh M. Taylor

Page Two

July 19, 1985

system and most of our borrowers report on a LIFO basis. The second reason for the lack of progress is pretty basic in that the Credit Department has only two personal computers available for spreading. It's hard to understand why the Credit Department should be thus limited where an operation like our Project Finance group has two and many of the other lending groups have one or more. If the ability to produce automated statements in volume is going to remain at two personal computers, it's pretty clear that "the automated Credit Department" will remain more form than substance.

It is also pretty clear that it is going to become increasingly difficult to monitor the quality of our loan portfolio effectively. This is of particular concern since, as the attached schedule shows,

> the percentage of our loans in the #4 category had risen from 18% in December 1981 the equivalent of 40% by June 30, 1985. In addition, Loan Review now reviews all unrated credits at the #4 meetings. Dollar wise, this means a five fold increase from $225,000,000 in 1981 to $1,247,000,000 now. When you add to that the complexity of many of the loans that have been made in the last 18 months, the inability to use more effective tools is a major concern as well as being extremely frustrating.

The head of the Credit Department fell into the trap of sales, and as these stories show, the Credit Department became less and less able to perform its true function. Although the FIFO/LIFO business was ultimately dropped, the attempts at its implementation delayed the automation of spreading financial statements, which would have benefited the entire analysis process. This was a further indication of bending administrative procedures for the sake of marketing.

Legality over Morality

Along with the erosion of credit standards came a more legalistic approach to the bank's lending agreements and obligations, which in some cases superseded the bank's moral obligations, a change in attitude Mr. Chapman would have abhorred. An example follows. Hollis, a small company owned by Georgia-Pacific, was engaged in distributing industrial supplies to companies in the lower quadrant of the country, principally in the southeast, with warehouses and distribution facilities stretching north into Colorado and west into Texas. Georgia-Pacific decided to sell Hollis to one of BNE's customers who operated a stationery distributor in Florida for a total of $16,000,000. This sum included repayment of working capital advances by Georgia-Pacific plus the purchase of the company's stock. The analysis was based on assumptions that Georgia-Pacific would continue to buy most of their industrial supplies from Hollis and that Hollis's management would stay with the company after the change in ownership. The investor was to invest $1,000,000 to purchase the equity, and Worthen Bank would finance the purchase of Hollis's rolling stock (vehicles used to deliver supplies) and, presumably, the balance of their equity. The Bank of New England facilities would be secured by the assignment of accounts receivable and inventories. In order to clear the funds received from the Hollis account debtors, a lockbox arrangement was set up at Worthen Bank. The checks would be sent to the lockbox account at Worthen Bank, and when deemed collected, Worthen would wire transfer the funds to BNE in Boston to apply to the loan—a typical arrangement.

The loan closings, atypically, were not simultaneous, and BNE made its loan, taking an assignment of all the assets, including the automotive equipment. Worthen subsequently made their loan to be secured by a lien on said equipment, a lien to which BNE had agreed to subordinate. Unbeknownst to the bank, the $1 million check that the new owner presented at the closing was actually covered by a check for $1 million he wrote out of working capital funds Hollis received at the closing. In essence, his contribution to the equity of the company was zero. Sometime later, the company filed for protection under Chapter 11 of the Bankruptcy Code, and the loan was transferred into the Controlled Loan Department at BNENA. Shortly after the loan had been transferred, Worthen Bank called the head of Loan Control to inquire about a subordination agreement that they had not received. Not finding it in the documentation, the head of Loan Control asked the former account officer's boss about it, and he confirmed that BNENA's attorneys, in fact, had drawn up the subordination agreement and had sent it to Boston for signature as the Customer Service Office did not have the authority to execute it. It turned out that the subordination agreement had been received in Boston but was never executed by the head of the Commercial Finance Department; when the question was asked whether or not the Worthen money "was in" and the answer was that the Worthen loan had indeed been made, the subordination agreement was deliberately ignored, effectively leaving Worthen in a secondary position on the automotive collateral rather than granting them the first position as agreed.

After making their loan, Worthen's follow-up had been lax, and they only realized that the subordination agreement was missing when they reviewed their documentation after Hollis had filed for bankruptcy under Chapter 7 of the Bankruptcy Code. Meanwhile, the trustee in bankruptcy had frozen all of the Hollis bank accounts—a routine procedure—including the lockbox account at Worthen Bank. When Worthen found out that the subordination agreement had never even been executed by Bank of New England, they immediately exercised their bank's right of set-off against the lockbox account upon release by the trustee. The amount of the set-off, although less than their loan, was close to $800,000 and was a good deal more than BNENA ultimately recovered when the fleet of cars and trucks was sold.

Loan Approval and Management

Playing the Loan Approval Process

The role of the bank lending officer or account officer has evolved from passively responding to requests for credit from potential borrowers—in essence that of order taker—to actively seeking potential lending opportunities and selling the bank's financial services, ranging from loans to lockboxes to custodial services for pension funds. The job is very similar to that of an insurance broker or stockbroker, and the income they receive in the form of salary and bonus reflects their ability to bring in business. This has brought about numerous changes in the manner in which loan requests are approved. Bank of New England moved from unlimited lending authority for lending officers, to graduated authority depending upon individual officers' training, experience, and lending skills, to graduated authority plus review by loan approval committees. Officers in the Loan Production Offices or Customer Service Offices, regardless of their titles or experience, had no lending authority.

Most banking institutions have an approval system that grants the account officers lending authority at various levels beyond which they must get an additional officer to sign off on the loan and, if the loan request is large enough, go one step further and present the request to a loan approval group. The loan approval group may consist of several senior officers in the "chain of command," each of whom must sign off on the proposal and who may be approached independently or in a group committee meeting. It is not unusual for the CEO of a bank to be the ranking member of the loan approval group. There are weaknesses attendant to every loan approval process, and it does not take the experienced lender very long to locate them. In the relatively simple dual-signature process, lenders tend to go to the officer they feel will be most sympathetic to the proposal, future reciprocity being an important factor in their selection. In the Loan Approval Committee procedure, the most senior officer to sign off should get the proposal last, but often the proposal is discussed and presented to him or her first, as senior approval virtually assures that of the rest of the group. Some committee procedures require votes from the committee members; again, in this case, the chairman of the committee should cast the last vote. Ideally, the vote should be by silent ballot, but most of them are vocal. The drawback to the oral vote is that committee members frequently do not want to be perceived as going against the tide and will cast their vote as they perceive the tide to be running, particularly if the chairman of the committee appears to have a preference.

"All those in favor say 'Aye.'"
"Aye." *"Aye."* *"Aye."* *"Aye."* *"Aye."*

Logic and equity would dictate that the most senior approval authority, whether individual or committee, be held responsible for the consequences of approval. There were several flaws in the bank's approval system stemming from the fact that the Senior Loan Approval Committee (or any divisional loan approval committee, for that matter) did not officially regard itself as other than a sounding board in spite of citing loans "approved by the Loan Approval Committee" in the monthly presentations to the Loan Review Committee of the board. In addition, it was perceived throughout the institution (including many district managers at the senior vice president level) as the most senior approval body. This was to be expected; not only did the committee name imply that role, but if it did not have the role, loans above assigned lending authorities could not have been made. The consequence was loss of accountability, and with that loss the quality of the loan portfolio inevitably suffered.

There was an interesting article published by Robert Morris Associates in an issue of *The Journal of Commercial Bank Lending* in the late 1980s. The article reported the results of a survey of bank officers, made by a Texas university professor, the focus of which was the behavior of loan approval committees. Each of the participants was given a separate loan proposal to evaluate and to either approve or turn down. They were unaware that all had received the same loan request. The results of the survey were kept confidential and reflected that the loan request had been unanimously rejected. The officers then met as a committee for the first time to consider what they assumed would be a new loan proposal but which was, in fact, the same one they had considered individually. The loan was approved unanimously. The conclusions the professor drew from the survey were that people in a group generally do not like to stray from the perceived group opinion, and most of them do not like to be seen as pessimists. They therefore temper their opinion to conform. This is particularly the case when no recorded votes are taken and the individual committee members are not held accountable for the consequences of their "joint" decisions.

Accountability vs. a "Sounding Board"

One of the biggest deficiencies of any loan committee approval system, whether meeting as a group or having a system under which loan proposals are circulated to the committee members individually, is that it separates loan responsibility from accountability. An example of this is to be found in the chapter entitled "Misapplied Principles," which cites the case of the loan to Hunt Energy, a start-up in Ohio. The loan was brought in by the Cleveland Customer Service Office, presented through the Commercial Finance Department in Boston, approved by the Senior Loan Approval Committee, and eventually resulted in a loss of some $10–$14 million. Shortly after the charge-off had been taken, a group of officers were having lunch in the cafeteria, among them being Tom Wilson, the head of the Commercial Banking Division. The issue of the Hunt Energy loss came up, and Wilson commented that the manager of the Commercial Finance Department really felt very badly about it. This prompted the comment that he must have cried all the way to the bank as he had, in fact, been promoted. No one in the Customer Service Office was disciplined, fired, or reprimanded. Apparently, nobody was held responsible. It is little wonder that a large segment of the lending staff felt neither responsibility nor accountability for the loans for which they were theoretically "responsible."

Those responsible for the various duties assigned to them, whether administrative or executive in nature, are the ones who must be held accountable for the consequences of the manner in which they discharge those duties. They must also be given the authority necessary to discharge their duties effectively. For example, the establishment of lending authorities (i.e., setting dollar limits beyond which the account officer or group leader must receive the approval of higher authority before a loan may be made) also establishes the limit on the officer's responsibility; the officer or group leader is to be regarded as being fully responsible for and held accountable for the consequences of loans made within the bounds of his or her loan approval authority. They are his or her responsibility. Those loans, which may only be made with the consent of higher authority, become, by definition, the responsibility of the higher authority consenting to the loan request. It is unrealistic to expect that an account officer or group leader should bear the responsibility for a bad loan in excess of his lending authority. The only exceptions to this would be those cases in which the account officer or group leader did, in fact, exceed his lending authority or those instances where adverse consequences occurred as a result of negligence or mismanagement of the loan by the account officer or group subsequent to the loan's approval. If mismanagement or negligence can be established, then both the group leader and his account officer should be held accountable for the consequences and disciplined accordingly. If the responsibilities are not being properly discharged by those individuals in the approval chain, then they should be removed from the approval process or the approval process itself should be appropriately changed. Unless corrective action is taken to address the issue raised by separation of responsibility and accountability, management of the loan portfolio is materially weakened, and the consequences can be severe.

Withholding of Reports

The members of the Loan Review Committee of the Board of Directors met on a monthly basis. The name of the committee would imply that they in some manner reviewed the entire loan portfolio to assure themselves that the risks remained at an acceptable level. This could be achieved in several ways, the most obvious being to have the manager of Loan Review Department report directly to that committee or, at a minimum, to have the committee hold periodic in-depth discussions with the head of the Loan Review Department and to review the reports the department generated. However, senior management felt otherwise, and the committee neither met with the head of the Loan Review Department nor received any of the reports the department generated. Instead, the scope of the Loan Review Committee's discussion at review was generally limited to three pieces of information: the loans approved during the month, loans that had been classified as workouts for the first time, and material changes in existing classified loans. Recommendations made by the heads of Loan Control and the Loan Review Department that the committee at least be provided the Loan Review Department reports were summarily dismissed. By withholding the reports, another of the many important elements of independent oversight was effectively eliminated.

Ambiguous Authorship and Ownership

One of the questions that came up from time to time at the monthly meetings of the Loan Review Committee was, "Who made this loan?" Although the classification write-up or "Controlled Loan memo" gave the name of the originating office and officer, it was, in a sense, a question without an answer. The personnel in our Customer Service Offices and Loan Production Offices had no lending authority for one thing, and typically the issue would be raised when the loan in question was large enough to exceed the lending authority of any individual officer, including division heads. Since the Loan Approval Committee did not assume any responsibility as an approval body and the loan exceeded individual authorities, who, indeed, "made the loan"? It was not uncommon for the answer to be concluded with the statement, "He's no longer with us" when the originating officer had left the bank. This answer was a misleading non sequitur, the implication being that the officer who "made the loan" had been fired. I know of none who were. Those who left did so of their own volition for better jobs with other financial institutions, in several cases testifying to that effect when litigation arose during the course of collection efforts. Inferring that officers had been fired when they had not was unethical and more than likely actionable if they had been aware of the allegations and chose to follow that course. In other cases, the answer to the "Who made this loan?" question was simply to give the name of the originating office (e.g., "the Cleveland office"). In either case, discussion of the role of the Loan Approval Committee in the decision to make the loan was not broached. The answers effectively distracted the Loan Review Committee's attention from the role the Senior Loan Approval Committee had played in the loan's approval. The ambiguity of the answers, deliberate or otherwise, internally cast a pall over their integrity.

Following is a copy of the memo written to the Credit Policy Officer.[17]

Bank of New England
Memorandum

To: Hugh M. Taylor, Executive Vice President

From: Charles B. M. Douglas, Senior Vice President

Re:

Date: September 24, 1985

My memo to you of September 23 covering the Hollis situation points to a problem that I believe is symptomatic of a deeper issue, that being the difficulty in clearly defining the responsibility of loan loss. Since the authority of the contact officer is limited and action that he takes requires the approval of his superiors, to discharge such an officer because of a loss incurred as a result of his approved actions is not only inequitable, it may well be actionable.

CDO0026

No action was taken to correct the situation, and the Senior Loan Approval Committee continued to dodge the question of collective responsibility.

Weaknesses Noted but Not Fixed

Oversight problems and improper loan management by the various lending groups were not addressed at Loan Review Committee meetings; the question of why the loans were allowed to deteriorate so far without corrective action was never addressed. The Loan Review Department and OIC Loan Control repeatedly pointed out weaknesses in departmental loan administration and procedures but had no authority to enforce any of the recommendations made in their reports to the Credit Policy Officer (who was also the head of Credit Administration) and in memos. A memo dated August 1, 1988, to the president reads in part:[18]

> The attached chart of our loans by risk rating is a combination of data obtained by the Loan Review Department in prior years and data now compiled for the Asset Quality Report. It clearly shows a migration of loan quality to the lower credit ratings. This is not entirely surprising given the competitive environment in the marketplace in recent years. It also indicates the tremendous growth in the size of the loan portfolio. What is not disclosed by the data is that: (1) the complexity of the loans has increased substantially, (2) lending specialties have grown to represent a significant percentage of the portfolio, (3) administrative

controls within the lending groups have slackened where they existed, or have simply failed to develop satisfactorily. The review of the Real Estate Department, for example, has confirmed again that administrative controls are sadly lacking. We were criticized by the bank examiners in 1985 for the condition of credit files in that department, but as we had undertaken a review of that department to determine the magnitude of the problem prior to the arrival of the examiners, the criticism was softened by a recognition that the problem was being addressed. While our review of the Real Estate credit files did indeed point out the magnitude of the problem, no definitive action was taken to correct it. Needless to say, the Real Estate portfolio has grown very aggressively in both volume and credit standards since, so that the problem has been greatly compounded. I am thoroughly convinced that our real grasp of the Real Estate portfolio is not as thorough as it should be and that an in-depth analysis of that portfolio might reveal serious weaknesses.

It is one thing to point out control weaknesses, it is another to implement effective change. I do not believe it can be done without a firm commitment to administrative change which would provide the implementation and maintenance of controls as opposed simply to control mechanism derivations. Although I cannot speak for the groups involved, it is my strong suspicion that market share growth and budgetary constraints combine in such a way

> that administrative control is in fact reduced as volume grows. When you consider that the percentage of our portfolio concentrated in loans rated 5 or worse has gone from 46% in 1985 to 59% in June of 1988, the consequences of weak administrative control can be disastrous.

In spite of the weaknesses pointed out and the potential for serious portfolio problems, there was no follow-up action.

Loan Approval Committee of One

The makeup of the Bank of New England Loan Approval Committee changed from time to time. In 1981, the Loan Approval Committee (LAC) was chaired by the Credit Policy Officer who remained as chairman when he was promoted to president of Bank of New England, NA (BNENA). When he was further promoted to chairman of BNENA, the executive vice president in charge of commercial banking was named president of BNENA and became chairman of LAC. Soon after, he established a new loan approval system so that each lending division would have its own loan approval committee to which all division loans between $1 million and $2 million would be presented. The committees consisted of the division manager as chairman, representatives from credit administration, and division officers. As with the former LAC, votes or sign-offs by anyone but the divisional LAC chairmen were not required for approval, so in theory, the system gave division heads a lending authority up to $2 million.

In practice, the divisional loan approval committees remained as mere sounding boards. All loans in excess of $2 million were presented to the Senior Loan Approval Committee (SLAC), its membership consisting of the president of BNENA (committee chair), the Credit Policy Officer, his assistant, the head of Loan Control, the head of Loan Review, and all the division heads. The Senior Loan Approval Committee members still did not vote or sign off on any proposal; they were expected to have read the analyses and to ask questions. The "tone" of the questions and the answers given by the presenter would be considered by the chairman of the committee, and he would make his decision as he saw fit. It was, in effect, a committee of one.

It was unusual for the chairman and some members to have read the analyses before the LAC meeting due to constraints on their time. Others were reluctant to raise what might be construed as critical questions on loans presented by other divisions lest their own proposals be criticized in turn; rather than appear to be negative, they chose to remain silent. Still others chose not to attend the meetings. Consequently, the number of committee members raising questions was very limited. The chairman could take the absence of questions by the silent members as tacit consent to the proposal, if he were so inclined. There were other deficiencies in the process as well. Loans were often "approved out of committee," which occurred fairly frequently with Real Estate proposals when the lending area manager could convince the SLAC chairman that the need to get back to the potential borrower left no time for a full analysis or a presentation to the committee.

Loan Review

Commercial banks were, in the 1980s (and probably still are), very highly leveraged, capital then making up only 6% of total footings, 94% being represented by deposit and other long-term obligations. Combined loans and discounts are the largest asset category on a commercial bank's balance sheet and consist primarily of commercial loans. The investment in the loans is supported by demand and time deposits, by funds borrowed from other institutions, by other long-term debt, and by equity. While all loans have some degree of risk, a bank's leverage makes it imperative that loan portfolio be monitored continually to enable timely corrective action to be taken.

The function of the Loan Review Department varies by bank. In those banks whose loan portfolios consist of a large number of relatively small loans, the function may be limited to a periodic review of loan documentation; in banks whose loan portfolios consist of larger commercial loans, the function is often the equivalent of that performed by bank examiners. The loan review function is the means by which bank management and managers of the various lending departments (e.g., Real Estate Department, Financial Institutions Department, etc.) can be kept informed of the quality of the loans, the effectiveness of loan management, and the degree of risk involved. A lawyer in the trust department of Irving Trust Company once quipped that his job was that of "keeping management's peckers out of the guillotine." While both his metaphor and his assumption of gender would be considered inappropriate today, the gist of that job description still applies to the head of the Loan Review Department. Under normal circumstances, the process itself should consist of periodic reviews of the loans in the loan portfolio by a group of experienced lending or analytically trained people who were not involved in the process of originating or approving said loans. The group also should review the administrative procedures followed by the various lending departments in managing their loans for laxness on the part of the lending officers in maintaining proper credit files, monitoring compliance with loan covenants, and maintaining records. At BNE, the review process initially had been a function of the Credit Department where financial statements submitted by existing and prospective borrowers were formally reviewed and analyzed. The written Credit Department analysis and customer's credit file then were sent to the officer responsible for the loan. Recommendations were not made by the Credit Department. The action to be taken, if any, was left up to the account officer to decide. A review of the loan portfolio was also made by the bank examiners, who took a statistical sampling of the portfolio for analysis during their periodic examinations of the bank. The loan review procedure was changed during the early 1960s with the establishment of the Loan Review Department, although the Credit Department continued its role in analysis of financial statements and pre-loan credit proposal write-ups.

As was pointed out in the chapter entitled "Loan Approval and Management," Loan Review officers are often regarded as negative critics by department heads and lending officers, with the result that the relationship between them is often strained rather than that of cooperation and appreciation for constructive criticism. Senior management is often composed of men and women who received their training in commercial lending and came up through the ranks as commercial lenders. Consequently, in some institutions there is a tendency for senior management to regard loan review criticisms with a certain amount of skepticism and with the suspicion that Loan Review Department reports and opinions tend to overstate the severity of problems. The senior management of Bank of New England chose to ignore the fact that an objective, unbiased evaluation of a large and diverse loan portfolio and the manner in which it is managed by the lending groups is essential if management of the institution is to understand the true quality of the portfolio. It was frequently pointed out that the loan portfolio had grown at an alarming rate and that the Loan Review Department had simply not kept pace with the increasing requirement for trained personnel. Citing budgetary constraints, the Credit Policy Officer delayed the approval of additional personnel; and when finally taken, the action was far short of the requirement. In an effort to improve relations between the Loan Review and Commercial Lending staff, the Credit Policy Officer further diluted the efficiency of the department by assigning extra tasks not normally assumed by Loan Review personnel. The following is an excerpt from a memo written to the head of Loan Control by Lawrence Kelley in October 1986 shortly after he joined Bank of New England to become the officer in charge of the Loan Review Department:[19]

> On several different occasions during the past few weeks, we have exchanged our mutual concern over the explosive growth of the corporate loan accounts, particularly as it relates to our responsibilities, i.e. loan quality. To date, existing policies and control features have worked very well in maintaining acceptable quality and I suspect that many of these same techniques will continue to manifest their effectiveness.
>
> However, in all candor, I feel very strongly that the philosophies, scope and approach of the Loan Review Department need to be altered if we are to meet the challenges that are now facing us. Many of the functions now fulfilled by the Loan Review Department are more in line with loan monitoring and credit support activity and provide little in the way of an early warning system. Further, the methods which we employ to carry out these duties appear to be fragmented to point where it is difficult to track accountability and manage resources.
>
> Such circumstances are not unusual in a dynamic growth environment like we are currently experiencing. The process evolved to meet immediate requirements and now needs

> to be revised in order to extract maximum efficiencies from our limited resources. In concert with these thoughts/opinions, I have attached an abbreviated set of Goals and Strategies developed as part of the recent budgeting process.
>
> In order to better establish the perspective from which I am coming, I think that is important that the loan review function be entirely independent. This is conceptually consistent with the Commercial Loan Manual which states that the "Loan Review Department is an independent reviewing entity responsible for assessing the quality of commercial loans and leases booked in the Bank of New England and its affiliates." I fully agree with this statement except that it could be expanded to embrace all credit risk within the Bank.
>
> In any event, the methods that we use in meeting this mission are not necessarily "independent" or "review" oriented. In fact out of a staff of twelve, I estimate that only 30% of the available time is spent on early warning efforts. We essentially provide a passive approach to loan review and react to known situations rather than assuming a proactive posture.

In the memo, Kelley pointed out that not only should existing procedures in reviewing the loan portfolio be changed to a proactive basis but also that existing staffing of the department was inadequate. The memo was discussed at length with the Credit Policy Officer, but again, no effective action resulted, the excuse being that increasing personnel was not in the budget.

The role of the bank examiners is to ensure that the assets in which depositors' funds are being invested and other areas of bank risk are being managed in a safe and sound manner. Examiners represent the government agencies that insure banks for the protection of their depositors and, as such, are obligated to report on all areas where they perceive weaknesses in order that corrective action may be taken by bank management or by bank regulators. While they review all areas where banking functions expose the institution to risk, one of their main focus points in most commercial banks is on the manner in which commercial loan transactions of all kinds are handled and the administrative procedures in place for proper risk management. The examiners' reports carry a great deal of weight with the comptroller of the currency and other bank regulators who have the authority to require what they perceive as appropriate corrective action to be taken. Failure to take action can have dire consequences for the institution and the management. On the other hand, examiners' negligence can result in continuation of substandard lending policies, erosion of credit standards, and abuses such as insider transactions. Failure on the part of examiners undoubtedly played a role in the horrific losses incurred by the savings and loan industry in the 1980s and by some commercial banks in the late 1980s and early 1990s.

Many commercial bank managements view the bank examiners as unwelcome and interfering critics who have no business telling them how to run "their" bank. A few examiners respond to the emotion by approaching the examination with an air of subjective hostility and others by softening their criticisms too far in an effort to be as inoffensive as possible. It is an unfortunate resentment for the examiners should serve and be accepted by management as valuable, objective resources in evaluating adherence to sound lending practices and in judging the managerial capacity of their subordinates.

Loan Ratings

The Merchants National Bank began to expand through acquisitions and mergers during the late 1950s and early 1960s, first acquiring the Pilgrim Trust Company in 1958 and later the New England Trust Company in the early 1960s. The loans assumed with the acquisition of the Pilgrim Trust Company were generally of a lower quality than the loans generated by the Merchants National Bank. A review of the Pilgrim portfolio was made by analysts in the Merchants National Bank Credit Department prior to the acquisition, and after the acquisition, the Merchants Credit Department assumed general supervision of credit analysis. It became apparent that some of the Pilgrim loans clearly were not being followed appropriately, with a commensurate increase in risk. It was decided that progress in risk reduction should be reported on a monthly basis to a committee (subsequently named the controlled loan committee) to make sure that corrective action was being taken. Those loans rated as 5 by the

Credit Department under the bank's new rating system were removed from the responsibility of the originating officers, and most were transferred to the Commercial Finance Department where collateral could be taken and closely monitored. As the bank grew during the 1960s and early 1970s, the Controlled Loan Committee was replaced by a Controlled Loan Department, and all loans presenting an unsatisfactory risk were transferred to that department.

With the growth and variation in customer base resulting from the acquisitions, it also became apparent that there was a need for a uniform risk rating system to be applied to all commercial loans, beginning with the initial credit analysis and updated every time the credit was analyzed—at least annually. The bank examiners used defined terms of *Satisfactory, Generally Satisfactory, Substandard, Doubtful*, and *Loss* in categorizing the loans they reviewed, and the bank decided to adopt a numerical rating system using similar definitions. Donald Blake, then head of the Credit Department, was given the task of designing and implementing the system. For the first time, numbers were used to clearly define five levels of risk acceptability. Some twenty-five years later, in the mid-1980s, the ratings were expanded from "1–5" to "1–9," allowing the bank to reflect more precisely, using the higher numbers, the degree of risk in the lower end of the portfolio. With the exception of the shipping loans, the higher-risk loans were handled by the Controlled Loan Department. Loan ratings were not static. If the risk increased for any reason, the account officer was responsible for reflecting the increased risk by lowering the rating on the scale. Conversely, if the borrower's financial condition improved, the rating was to be upgraded. If properly maintained by the account officers and the Credit Department and confirmed by the Loan Review Department, the rating system would always reflect the risk level of the portfolio accurately. It would also be an important mechanism for estimating losses and the setting of the loan loss reserve.

Blake defined the ratings well, taking into consideration the financial characteristics specific to the nature of the businesses and industries in which the borrowers operated. At the time of its adoption, the system was regarded as "visionary," according to Lawrence Kelley, the former bank examiner who became the head of Loan Review in 1986. In time, the system was used as the basis for estimating losses and as a component of the calculation for determining the quarterly loan loss reserve. Logically, if the ratings were properly applied, all of the loan losses would emanate from the loans in the 6, 7, 8, and 9 categories, all of which would be handled as "controlled loans." Unfortunately, the lending staff did not regard very seriously their responsibility for properly maintaining the ratings of their loans, and many were not properly trained in the use of the new rating system, with the result that rating changes by account officers were very rare. For all practical purposes, account officers concentrated on marketing efforts, and ratings were only changed when the Credit Department analyzed a borrower's financial statements or when the files were reviewed by the Loan Review Department.

The loan portfolio grew substantially over the years, and in 1980, the various segments of the total portfolio were assigned to various officers in the Loan Review Department for monitoring; but because the number of personnel in the loan review function had not kept pace, their interim reviews consisted primarily of spot checks of credit files and periodic meetings. These ninety-day meetings were held for the purpose of reviewing the 5-rated loans and were attended by the head of Loan Control, the head of the Loan Review Department, the department manager whose loans were the subject of the review, his or her division manager, and the Loan Review officer nominally responsible for the departmental review. The department manager commented on any loans whose rating had been changed since the prior ninety-day review and on the status of each of the other 5-rated loans in his portfolio. By far the greatest numbers of rating changes were made by the Credit Department when they performed their annual review of financial statements submitted by the borrowers and occasionally as a result of the ninety-day reviews. Loan Review officers would occasionally recommend downgrading of particular loans to the head of the Loan Review Department, who had the authority to change any rating with which he disagreed. Downgrading a rating by the account officers handling the loans or by department managers was uncommon. Toward the end of the 1980s, management decided that each account officer would be held responsible for maintaining proper ratings of the loans in his or her portfolio and be judged, in part, by the accuracy of their ratings. As pointed out in the chapter entitled "Measurements of Management Effectiveness," however, pressure was often brought on the head of the Loan Review Department by group leaders and the chairman of the Loan Approval Committee to improve the ratings of loans that had been adversely rated by Loan Review. The action, of course, had the opposite effect on management's stated effort to hold the account officers responsible for maintaining objective ratings on their own loans—why should they be held to a standard that senior management's actions undercut?

Differences in Expectations and Training of Workout Officers

As was stated earlier, bank lending officers are basically hired to sell a bank's financial services, and they receive fairly basic training in financial analysis as a means of educating them about the nature of the products they are expected to sell. In a broad sense, their objective is to do whatever it takes to please the customer. As might be expected, successful lending officers generally are extroverted, put a favorable "spin" on their proposals, and focus on the positive aspects when selling the proposals both to the customer and internally to whatever lending authority is required. This is not done with the intent to deceive but rather results from having earnestly convinced themselves of the merits of the proposals. As long as these tendencies are acknowledged, they can be channeled by the section head or group leader in a very positive and productive manner. When it comes to loan collection, however, those traits that make a good salesman are far less important than the ability to determine the causes for the deterioration and to address both the customer and the problem effectively so as to minimize a bank's exposure. He or she must be able to make the borrower understand that his interests are now subordinate to the efforts of the bank to improve its protection and convince the borrower on what action must be taken by the borrower in order to accomplish that objective. Sometimes this is readily accomplished; at other times, it is a real challenge. For example, in the mid-1970s, Irving Trust Company was the lead bank in a multimillion revolving credit extended to TWA. Since the airline had been experiencing difficulties for some time, it was under close scrutiny by both office head and loan administration. Many of the troubled loans were left in the hands of the office head in whose office the loan was being handled. The TWA loan was housed in the 245 Park Avenue office, and so it fell to me as office head to handle. I requested that we be collateralized by a security interest in the airline's aircraft. The company treasurer understood my position and approached the airline chairman, Charles Tillinghast, with the proposal. Tillinghast said he could not agree because if the company were to give the banks security, they would be tempted sell off the aircraft to pay off the loan. When the treasurer got back to me with that answer, I said that the fear was foolish as it would be the same as flying in an airplane wearing a parachute and being tempted to jump out the window to see if it would open. The treasurer laughed, and we were subsequently given the collateral. Contrast this with a borrower who had given a second mortgage on his home as additional collateral on his business loan. When foreclosure procedures began, he took an ax and methodically went through the house hacking holes in all the walls, ceilings, and floors, a final display of defiance. Clearly the customer refused to accept his own responsibility for his predicament.

The training and orientation or focus of the lending officers has to balance judiciously between the needs and interests of the bank and the needs and interests of the borrowers. The good account officer is usually an extrovert, whereas the good workout officer tends to be more objective, more skeptical, and more analytical. Both require an ability to deal with people effectively, but the workout officer faces the additional task of entering a relationship that has, in many instances, already turned hostile and having to persuade the borrower that his past behavior resulted in the current unsatisfactory status, that the pattern of behavior will have to change, and that mutual cooperation in solving what has become a mutual problem is the way the relationship will have to be handled.

In addition, the account officer must know what limitations are placed on a lender's behavior in order to avoid incurring lender liability. Bank management and government regulators very frequently make the mistake of assuming that an experienced lender will automatically make a good workout officer. The concept is as flawed as assuming that a good salesman will automatically make a good bill collector. Being an excellent account officer on the selling side does not translate into being a competent officer for dealing with troubled loan situations. A workout officer's training is far more varied, extensive, and intensive than that of an account officer, requiring full understanding of the financial dynamics of borrowers in different industries, the legal implications of actions taken or recommendations made to the borrower, and the bank's rights and its obligations to the borrower. The rigor of these requirements and procedures is evidenced in the table of contents of the "Work Out Department Policies and Procedures Guide."[20]

Work Out Department Policies and Procedures Guide

Table of Contents

4.5	C.	Use of Contract Labor
4.8	D.	Lender Liability
4.13	E.	In Substance Foreclosure
4.13	F.	Troubled Debt Restructuring

Slow Reaction to the Developing Crisis

As can be seen by glancing through the manual contents, competent management of the workout process demands of the individual workout officer far more legal and practical knowledge than that typically possessed by even the well-experienced loan officer. Improper handling can result in increased loss and in lender liability for abuse of borrower rights and improper handling of collateral. At BNENA, for example, the workout of bad shipping loans was left in the hands of those responsible for making them in the first place and sometimes resulted in losses in amounts in excess of the original loans. For management to believe that lending officers can be readily transferred into the workout function to meet any emergency that may arise is naïve and merely reflects the lack of understanding of what the workout job entails. While assurances were made that experienced lending officers would be transferred into the Controlled Loan Department to assist if needed, repeated requests for additional personnel, either new hires or transfers into the Controlled Loan Department, were denied on the basis of budgetary constraints. In 1988, the volume of identified troubled loans began to grow rapidly, and there were not enough experienced workout people to handle them; the people transferred into the Controlled Loan Department needed more supervision than the workout group leaders could adequately give, and the department was simply overwhelmed. Accurate risk assessment of the loans, beyond the ratings assigned by Loan Review at the time of transfer, simply could not be achieved by the new account officers. It reached the point where the transfer into the department of newly classified loans was put on hold as it is always better to have a troubled loan receive attention from the originating officer than to receive no attention whatsoever. The slow reaction to the developing crisis by the BNENA Credit Policy Officer and his superiors in the late 1980s was brought about by their lack of experience in the workout area and lack of understanding of the complexities involved in doing an effective workout job. The eventual action taken was too little, too late.

Differences in Workout Loan Practices

The growth in the volume of troubled loans required regulatory agencies as well as banks to staff up in the departments responsible for handling them. The managers hired by the regulators to manage loans for them were frequently former bank lending officers from failed banks with no workout experience, many located well out of the geographical area where the bulk of their assigned loans were located. The Resolution Trust Corporation (established by the federal government to handle the liquidation of the assets of defunct savings and loan institutions in the 1980s), for example, hired management firms ranging from Pennsylvania to Texas to manage pools of loans in New England. Because of this, they had a tendency to make decisions that were not in the public's best interests. There are two theories for handling workout loans, one being to work with the borrower to improve the situation while strengthening whatever collateral position is available, and the other is simply to force liquidation of the collateral or to sell the loan to another lender or investor at a deep discount. Due to these new regulators' inexperience with troubled loans, the latter was the route they strongly advised. In many cases, the contractors refused (or did not have the authority) to renew past-due loans that had been written with five-year maturities and twenty-year amortization rates, loans that could have continued to be performing had they been renewed for another period at the original amortization rates. As nonperforming loans, they sold for a fraction of what they could have received had they been sold as performing loans. In addition, the obligations having been sold as nonperforming loans, the borrowers often faced foreclosure by new holders of their notes who wanted only to maximize their return as quickly as possible. Real estate projects that were under construction were not only not completed but frequently left with no security with the result that they were completely vandalized and, for all practical purposes, abandoned. Any value that may have been there was completely lost. Legally, the borrower is entitled to the fair market value of pledged collateral, and if the value of the collateral deteriorates as a direct result of action or inaction by the lender, the lender is liable to the borrowers for the decline. (See Workout Manual section III, "Enforcement of the Bank's Rights.") Even if possession of the collateral has not been taken, common sense would dictate that appropriate steps be taken to preserve or enhance the value of the pledged collateral. For example, common sense would dictate that a construction project near completion would sell for more if completed than it would if all construction were ceased, the property not secured to the weather or against vandalism, for all practical purposes, abandoned for an extended period. There are many instances where funding was suspended by the contractors for the FDIC or RTC for projects near completion. Rather than advance the funds necessary for proper securitization of the projects, they were essentially abandoned with the result that the projects lacking security were severely vandalized and became worthless before the time came for disposition. A very substantial portion of the BNE loans handled by BNE personnel for the FDIC were sold off at a large discount in "packages" of several loans rather than trying to improve the inherent risk.

Misapplied Principles

But It's Traditional Practice!

The word *tradition* is defined in Webster's Dictionary as [1] the handing down of information, beliefs, and customs by word of mouth from one generation to another without written instruction and [2] an inherited pattern of thought or action." Once a new industry has become well-established, as with the larger society and culture of which it is an integral part, it tends to rely on tradition instead of innovation. This tendency serves a variety of social and practical purposes, including safety (risk aversion) and comfort (adhering to familiar practice rather than setting precedents). The banking industry at its inception was successful because of its conservatism—its reliance on the tried and true. "Traditional banking practice" became synonymous with "acceptable levels of risk." For many decades, the banking field attracted people not for their entrepreneurial and salesmanship skills but rather for their perceived analytical abilities and common sense. As the financial opportunities changed, multiplied, and diversified, rather than questioning and consciously developing new sets of assumptions, a curious thing happened. Bank personnel from junior account officers to presidents recommended and accepted outrageous loan proposals if presented as "traditional banking practice" even if they were not. The description alone apparently was enough to send the message, however erroneous, of palatable risk. Consequently, it is not unusual to have certain aspects of requested loans described as traditionally acceptable in bank or industry practice when, in fact, nothing approaching a traditional acceptance of those aspects exists. By the same token, it is not unusual to interpret what really is traditional practice in a way that justifies behavior that is not traditional. This can lead lending administrators and account officers to extrapolate what may be sound principles for lending to one type of borrower to borrowers with only very superficial similarities and without regard for the limited basis supporting the extrapolation. Misapplied principles can be extremely costly, as is illustrated below.

Project financing is a term generally applied to financing drilling and developing of gas and oil fields by lending against the value of proven reserves of producing wells, where the sale of the gas or oil under contract provides the wherewithal for repayment of the loan. It allows the owner to replace the funds spent in development of producing properties and to invest those funds in further development. Project financing is used where the borrower has "take or pay" contracts with strong buyers and where proven reserves are sufficient to provide product in more than sufficient quantity to meet the contract terms. "Take or pay" contracts were made with gas- or oil-producing firms, under which they agreed to pay for a given dollar amount of gas or oil to meet the loan payment requirements and to make the payments whether any product was taken or not; and the principle has proven sound over many, many years of financing the oil and gas industry.

"That Pipe Deal"

A loan request was brought in by the Commercial Finance Customer Service Office in Cleveland to finance Hunt Energy, a company established to capitalize on the shortage of drilling pipe for the oil industry. The principal of the company had only superficial knowledge of the industry and had previously gone bankrupt in another type of venture. The manufacturing operations were to be conducted in a plant that had been abandoned by Youngstown Sheet and Tube. Hunt Energy was to purchase "state-of-the-art" continuous casting equipment manufactured abroad (and never before assembled or used in the United States) for making "oil country grade" seamless steel drilling pipe. The equipment was to be installed by a large engineering firm, and the pipe produced was to be sold to strong purchasers under contracts that called for quantities of pipe in sufficient amount and price to repay the $16,000,000 loan incurred to fund the purchase of the plant, equipment, and operating expenses. The chairman of the Loan Approval Committee, at the time the Credit Policy Officer, supported and approved the request, likening it in principle to a project finance loan simply because there were contracts in place to take the pipe when produced. The underlying principle of "proven reserves of producing wells and firm take-or-pay contracts for known output with strong buyers" that provides a sound basis for project financing was completely prostituted. After the meeting broke up, one of the account officers in the Boston Commercial Finance Department asked how the committee could possibly have approved "that pipe deal." As it turned out, the deliveries and installation of the equipment were so delayed and so problematic that the company was never able to produce the quality and amount of pipe originally planned. The first group of buyers backed out before signing their final contracts, and the company found others, albeit much weaker substitutes. Production was so delayed that even subsequent contracts were voided prior to any deliveries; the company filed for protection under Chapter 11, and about $12 million of our initial $16 million was a total loss.

"Here it is—the plain, unvarnished truth. Varnish it."

BNENA ultimately suffered staggering losses as a result of having extrapolated public utility financing principles, first to the CATV industry and then to radio broadcasting, paging, and movie theater chains, where the characteristics of CATV cash flow at that time had only superficial similarities to public utilities' cash flow pattern; the rest of the markets entered by the communications group had none. As stated in the October 14, 1987, memo to David G. Falwell, cited earlier, the communications group covered[21]

> CATV, radio, TV broadcasting, paging companies and bill board companies. While these have a Common characteristic, the transmission of information to a large public, their financial characteristics are different enough to make assuming too many similarities dangerous. Analysis of these companies focuses on cash flows rather than the more usual credit factors and the analytical work is handled by a limited number of trainees "specializing" is this area. The analysts depend upon the members of the Communication Group to provide them with industry trends, standards, characteristics and acceptable financing practice because there is no other ready source for the information. The trouble is that, other than for CATV, the group's members themselves are not really knowledgeable enough to be able to provide objective and appropriate information because of the recency of their own exposure to the segment of the industry addressed. The department, however, dominates the analysts and the analyses reflect it.

In spite of the significant differences between banking's traditional business with the utility industry, BNENA and other banks went blithely ahead without questioning their assumptions and tailoring their lending policies and practices accordingly. The prevailing attitude seemed to be "Everyone is doing it, so it must be all right." During the 1970s, one of the bank examiners criticized as substandard a REIT loan in which the bank participated since the cash flow simply was not there to provide adequate coverage. When he sat down with the manager of the Real Estate Department to discuss this rating, the manager objected, but the rating stuck, and the examiner returned to his office. Subsequently, the manager of the Real Estate Department came into the bank examiner's office and said, "Don't you realize that the Chase Manhattan Bank is the agent on this credit?" But clearly, in retrospect, it wasn't all right to accept another bank's decision without making a proper evaluation of one's own.

I was the head of the Wall Street District II office of the Irving Trust Company in 1970. The office specialized in serving the investment bankers and brokers by financing commercial transactions they brought to us. One such incident involved a request for a $10 million line of credit to a REIT. I approached Mr. Edward Wilson, my boss, with the request, and he replied that REITs were involved in lending money to real estate developers who did not meet standard bank credit criteria and that if we were unwilling to lend money to the developers directly, why should we be interested in lending money to those who, in turn, loaned it to borrowers unacceptable to us? I asked whether it would be acceptable if we were able to approve any investment made by the REIT that involved the use of our line of credit, to which he replied that that would be okay, but he seriously doubted that the REIT would agree. They did not agree to the limitation, and the request for the line of credit was withdrawn. The REIT movement of the 1970s was similar in many respects to the explosive growth of the CATV/communications business, in that banks went along with ever-reducing credit standards simply because other banks were doing it. The idea of banks accepting as sound what others appear to be doing successfully is neither unique nor limited to the past. A good example of the principle is the current crisis generated by excessive financing of subprime borrowers, where banks "warehoused" the loans made by nonbank lenders until the loans could be grouped and "securitized," the "securities" then sold to investors attracted by the rates of return, many of them being banks both here and abroad. As rates increased on mortgage loans, the subprime borrowers defaulted, and the market for them dried up. Those banks "warehousing" the unsold mortgages and the investors in the securities suffered large losses. An excerpt from the *Christian Science Monitor* dated August 17, 2007, carried the story:[22]

MORTGAGE LOANS held overseas have quadrupled since 2000.

By RON SCHERER
STAFF WRITER

NEW YORK–Over the past six years, Chinese central bankers, French pension-fund managers, and staid German bankers have been the piggy bank for America's housing boom.

In that time, foreign loans to help Americans get mortgages have quadrupled to nearly $1 trillion.

> That's one reason soaring foreclosure rates in the US and a sharp slump in the housing market have rattled traders from Frankfurt au Main in Germany to Pitt Street in Sydney, Australia. The prospect of large losses has caused stock markets to tumble worldwide. And central banks have injected billions of dollars to prevent a credit crunch from becoming a financial rout...

No Use Crying Over Spoiled Meat

Misapplied principles and concepts can be a hazard in just about any form of business. For example, a technique for marketing a line of products might be inappropriately applied to another line with superficial similarities but material differences. A case in point that comes to mind is that of a company in Chicago that was engaged in distributing meat products to retailers and had been doing so for one hundred years. The second-generation owner was ninety years old when he turned the reins over to his son. At that point, they were approached by an account officer at our Customer Service Office, who persuaded him to switch his financing to us. A warning point, raised but ignored because of the company's long success record, was that the son had recently managed an unrelated company into insolvency. The son, applying the principle of tie-in sales common in the distribution of dissimilar but complementary products, decided to expand sales by selling processed meats through refrigerator and freezer retailers, including a meat package option inside the appliances. The theory was that when the appliances had been sold and the meat package had been eaten, they would order more of the same to replenish the larder. Although a marked change in their traditional method of selling meat, it made sense superficially because housewives buy refrigerators and freezers and also buy frozen meats, and in addition, there was the implied endorsement of the meat products by the retailer. A lot of Sears stores and others signed up to go along. The initial stocking orders were very high, and sales to distributors expanded very quickly. Unfortunately, the retailers found that the meat could not be kept cold enough in their storage areas, and it all spoiled, literally turning black. The retailers were furious and refused to pay for the meat. The company very nearly went into bankruptcy. Since we had financed the receivables and a great many disappeared when the meat spoiled, we threatened to sue the guarantor, who was the ninety-year-old father. Luckily, the old man prevailed on some old friends who helped him transfer the loan to a Chicago bank, and we never had to go to court. We were not privy to the arrangements the old man made with his business friends, but the logical course would have been to sell out based on the reputation the company had with its traditional lines of distribution.

"Schmoozing" Corporate Policy

Consistent Application of Credit Policies

In 1988, David Falwell, the executive vice president and Credit Policy Officer for Bank of New England, was made CPO for the Bank of New England Corporation as well as for the Boston bank. In that capacity, it was his responsibility to make sure that credit policies at all of the affiliated banks were being interpreted in the same manner and to announce changes in policy as they occurred. One such change was that the management of all controlled loans in the Massachusetts affiliates would be the responsibility of the Controlled Loan Department at Bank of New England, Boston. All loans above $2,000,000 were to be under the supervision of the Controlled Loan Department, and all of those below $2,000,000 were to be handled by the newly created Community Banking

Controlled Loan Department. The changes at issue were fairly significant and a marked departure from both prior credit and personnel policy. The following communication to Richard Alden, then president of Bank of New England, North is a copy of one of the letters that were sent.

February 24, 1989

Mr. Richard L. Alden, President

BANK OF NEW ENGLAND-NORTH

61 Merrimack Street

Lowell, MA 01853

Re: Community Banking Controlled Loan Policies and Procedures

Dear Dick:

As we discussed, I am outlining below the procedures which are being followed for the Controlled Loan Departments of the Community Banks. You will note that the policies and procedures closely follow those in the Commercial Loan Manual and the practices followed at BNE, NA, and confirm our discussions of the manner in which we are implementing the policy.

I. Staffing:

1. Each of the Eastern Massachusetts Community Banks will establish a Controlled Loan Department to handle all of the loans

designated as Controlled Loans by virtue of risk rating or special handling requirements.

The staffing level required for each Controlled Loan Department will be determined by the OIC Community Banking Controlled Loans.

Staff members of each Controlled Loan Department will be employees of their respective banks, but all terms relating to their assignment/employment in the department as well as their titles, pay grades and evaluations will be determined by the OIC of each Controlled Loan Department and by the OIC Community Banking Controlled Loans. The OIC of each Controlled Loan Department will report directly to the OIC Community Banking Controlled Loans on all matters.

Controlled Loan Department account officers will be expected to remain in the department for a period of two years; assignments of shorter or longer duration will depend upon the needs of the department as determined by the OIC Community Banking Controlled Loans. It is assumed that account officers will return/transfer to available positions in the regular lending areas of their respective community banks upon completion of their assignments. It should be noted, however, that those who successfully complete their assignments also would be considered highly attractive candidates for available positions in the regular lending areas or Controlled Loan Departments of other BNE Banks.

It is expected that the Senior Loan Officer and other managers will actively encourage appropriate candidates to seek rotational assignments in the Controlled Loan Department; however, staff members will be transferred into the Controlled Loan Department or hired from outside the Bank only after having been screened and approved by the OIC Controlled Loan Department and the OIC Community Banking Controlled Loans.

2. The OIC Controlled Loan Department and the OIC Community Banking Controlled Loans will be designated as officers of both BHE,NA and of the Community Bank in question in order to enable them to conduct business relating to both "Legal Entity" and "Transfer Branch" (a/k/a "N.A.") controlled loan relationships.

II. Procedures:

1. Separate responsibility centers will be established to house each Community Bank's "Legal Entity" and "Transfer Branch" controlled loan relationships. The OIC Controlled Loan Department and the OIC Community Banking Controlled Loans will be granted all appropriate signing authorities to enable them to conduct business relating to both portfolios. Personnel and other

expenses will be charged to the Legal Entity responsibility center.

2. All loans rated "7" or worse by the originating lending group or by the Loan Review Department, and all loans classified as substandard or worse by state or federal bank examiners automatically are transferred to the Controlled Loan Department for handling.

   All loans rated "6" for more than six months either must qualify for upgrading and be upgraded by Loan Review or be transferred to the Controlled Loan Department. Exceptions to this policy may be granted by the Senior Loan Officer or the OIC Community Banking Controlled Loans provided that a complete analysis justifying the temporary waiver of policy accompanies the request. Such temporary waivers should not be granted for periods exceeding 90 days.

   Account officers, Group Leaders and Division Heads may recommend that a rated "5" or better, or rated "6" for fewer than six months loan be transferred to Controlled Loan for special handling, but such loans only will be transferred with the consent of the OIC Controlled Loan Department and OIC Community Banking Controlled Loans.

   The Loan Review Department may recommend the immediate transfer of any loan to Controlled Loan if it is rated "6" or worse.

3. All requests for account transfers to Controlled Loan must be in writing in a thoroughly-completed "New Controlled Loan Memo" (sample enclosed), prepared either by the account officer or Loan Review, with the original to be sent to the OIC Controlled Loan Department and copies to be sent to the OIC Loan Review, OIC Community Banking Controlled Loans, and to the OIC Loan Review and OIC Loan Control at BNE, NA.

4. If any loan is transferred to Controlled Loan, all other relationships having ownership common to the borrower in question also should be transferred to Controlled Loan together with all related deposit accounts.

   All Controlled Loans in excess of $2.0MM will be reviewed by the OIC Loan Control at BNE, NA to determine whether the loan should be transferred to Boston for handling. If the handling of the loan is left in the community bank, it will be handled by the community bank's Controlled Loan Department.

5. All releases from the Controlled Loan Department must be in writing by the Controlled Loan account officer and be approved by the OIC Controlled Loan, OIC Community Banking Controlled Loans, the OIC Loan Control, and the division head of the receiving lending group.

Once a loan has been transferred to the Controlled Loan Department, approval of a ny modifications, increases, etc. will be granted by the OIC Controlled Loan and/ or OIC Community Banking Controlled Loans, OIC Loan Control or Credit Policy Officer BNE,NA in accordance with their approval authority, without presentation to any LAC. Please note that the systems are not yet in place to enable us to establish this structure of approval authorities at the different Community Banks. Accordingly, while Controlled Loan's exemption from LAC has been implemented, the signature(s) of Community Bank Senior Loan Officers and/or Bank Presidents will be required to enable transactions to be booked by Loan Operations until further notice.

I hope the outline above clears up most of the questions you might have regarding the implementation of the centralized controlled loan policy. I would, of course, be glad to discuss any aspects of it with you in greater detail at your convenience.

Sincerely,

Charles B. M. Douglas
Senior Vice President
OIC Loan Control
CBMD/ljp
enclosure

The letter indicates the complexity of the proposed changes in some of our lending policies. As these changes were to be applied throughout Bank of New England Corporation, it was essential that each bank affected by the proposed changes understood the impact they would have on their operating procedures. In order for the application to be applied consistently throughout, there was no effective means of communication other than in writing. Not only would the written documents be consistent throughout, they also would serve as a point of reference when implementing the changes.

Censure of Policy Documentation as Unfriendly

The change was a practical way of applying much-needed oversight to the smaller troubled loans by having workout personnel reporting and responsible to people in Boston as well as to their own management. Lack of written clearly articulated policy opens the door for individual interpretations, some of which may not be those intended by the framers of the policy, and to excuses for the lack of any implementation at all. Concerned that the move could be structurally and politically awkward to implement, as some of the affiliated bank officers might interpret the move as an infringement on their authority, the head of Loan Control planned a visit with each of the Massachusetts affiliates to introduce the Boston personnel to the senior management of the affected banks. The first visit was with the president of Bank of New England, Essex. We explained how we planned to handle the loans from an operational standpoint. When we finished, the president looked at us and said the idea was fine but that he knew nothing about it. He said that although a meeting attended by the senior management of each of the Bank of New England Corporation banks had been held within the prior two weeks, things had been covered only in a broad, general sense with nothing of particular note. Nothing at all had been brought up about any change in credit policy or procedures. He asked to be provided something in writing detailing any changes in credit policy, and I did so upon returning to the office in Boston. In meetings with the other affected banks, senior managers were informed of the changes and told that they all would be receiving letters outlining the new policy and procedures.

After the letter to the Bank of New England, Essex, a meeting was held with the Credit Policy Officer to discuss the meeting with Essex and other banks, and he was shown a copy of the letter Essex had requested and which had been sent to the senior managements of the other affected banks. He became very upset and said he wished no letters had been sent out because, in his words, "I would rather schmooze things like this through." He went on to say that he had not brought the matter up at all at the management meeting because he fully intended to implement these and all formal changes in corporate policy in his own way. He added, "You don't understand, 90 percent of a senior manager's responsibility is to get along with other senior managers, and things like this should be done in a friendly, one-on-one, word-of-mouth manner." He sincerely believed this to be the case, and it didn't seem to occur to him that corporate policies of a multibillion dollar corporation cannot be left to purely subjective interpretation because changes in policy transmitted only by word of mouth to individuals in different parts of the corporation would be very difficult to track for uniform, correct interpretation and for compliance.

Resistance Overlooked

Another meeting was held with the Senior Credit Officer for Bank of New England, Worcester, who happened to be a friend of the Credit Policy Officer, to discuss the change in policy. The bulk of their workout loans were below the $2,000,000 level and, therefore, were to be managed under the jurisdiction of the Community Controlled Loan Department. Unfortunately, the Senior Credit Officer in Worcester had a personality conflict with the head of the Community Controlled Loan Department. Resentful of the perceived incursion into his authority, after our meeting, he complained to the Credit Policy Officer in Boston that we had insisted on his hiring a specific number of people in Worcester to handle the loans. The Credit Policy Officer brought the subject up at one of our frequent meetings, indicating that perhaps we had been too insistent on hiring more personnel in Worcester. I pointed out that nobody had insisted on *any* level of staffing since we had no idea of the size of the portfolio to be classified for inclusion in the workout category and therefore had no idea of the number of people needed to handle the portfolio. It was clear that the Worcester Senior Loan Officer was simply making an erroneous claim, to which the CPO commented, "I didn't think you had done that." I subsequently wrote a letter to the officer in Worcester pointing out that we had had no basis for insisting on certain personnel levels since we had no feeling for the size of the portfolio of loans involved. A copy of the letter was sent to the Credit Policy Officer. In a subsequent telephone conversation I had with the Worcester officer, he didn't disagree with anything in the letter but simply said, "So what? It's just your word against mine." I reported this to the Credit Policy Officer, who just shook his head. No action was ever taken, thereby diminishing the likelihood of any possibility of a relationship of good faith with the management of the Worcester bank. I related the story to Richard Driscoll, then chairman of BNENA, and showed him a copy of the letter in March 1989 when we discussed my decision to leave the bank. Symptomatic of management's failure to provide leadership, problem resolution, and discipline, his response was that the vice president in charge of the Community Banking Controlled Loan Department might be "turning out some lights out there," and apparently, he let it go at that. The impact on corporate policy acceptance and the greater corporate good seemed not to have been considered. Instead of a reprimand, the individual was later promoted.

PAST PERFORMANCES
WERE NO INDICATION
OF FUTURE RESULTS
Modell

Orphaned Portfolios

Prior to the merger with Connecticut Bank and Trust Corp. and Conifer Group, the New England Merchants National Bank Corp. had acquired several smaller banks in the state of Massachusetts, including the Cape Ann National Bank in Gloucester, Massachusetts, and the Bay State Merchants National Bank of Lawrence. In anticipation of the acquisition by the New England Merchants National Bank (NEMNB) holding company of CBT and the Conifer Group of banks, six of the existing eastern affiliate banks were merged into Bank of New England, NA in Boston in June 1986. The group of merging banks included both Cape Ann National Bank and the Bay State Merchants National Bank. The employees of each became employees of NEMNB. Their operations functions were consolidated into the Loan Operations Department of the New England Merchants National Bank. General oversight of the lending functions was assigned to a senior vice president in Boston, although direct management of the loans remained at the local level.

The Cape Ann National Bank and the Bay State Merchants National Bank had served the North Shore area, primarily with a variety of small commercial loans to local businesses and manufacturers and real estate loans to small store owners, small strip mall developers, and small real estate developers. While the total dollar amount of the combined loan portfolios was roughly $50 million, the number of borrowers was large. At the time of the merger, the president of the Cape Ann National Bank felt his talents were greater than what was required to manage a small subsidiary operation, and since he was well known and respected in the local communities, he left the bank to start a new bank in the area. When he left, he took virtually all of the experienced personnel with him to the new bank, leaving what had been his old operation bereft of people to handle the loan portfolio. The president of the Lawrence bank left to become the CEO of a bank in Maine, and many of the experienced lending personnel were hired away by other local institutions. The departure of experienced personnel resulted in what could best be described as grossly undermanaged portfolios in the market areas covered by the two merged banks.

Someone Else's Account

Lending officers in banks naturally tend to develop a proprietary interest in the loans they originate and in loans originated by departments under their leadership. Merger-mandated transfers of responsibility for loans originated by other institutions often result in neglect.

Account officers and their department managers simply do not feel "responsible" for transferred portfolios and therefore concentrate their attention on their own loans and in generating their own new business, in the belief that their performance will not be judged by the credit quality of inherited loans. Consequently, customers making up the transferred portfolios are treated by loan officers and managers alike as "someone else's account." They are often completely ignored. After the merger of the Patriot Bank portfolios into the Bank of New England, Boston portfolios, the former Senior Credit Officer at Patriot Bank was transferred into the Credit Administration Division. Sometime after the portfolio of real estate loans had been assumed by the Real Estate Department, I mentioned to him that the Patriot portfolio was showing some signs of severe strain, to which he replied, "When the Patriot real estate loans were transferred over to BNE, they represented a perfectly good portfolio of small loans. I have watched that portfolio deteriorate into a pile of shit for lack of attention." This lack of ownership by the new account officers means that information in the credit files is not kept up to date, loan covenants are not policed, financial statements are not requested, received financial statements are not reviewed or spread in a timely manner (if at all), interest payments fall behind, insurance policies expire without renewal, personal contact with the borrowers, if any, is infrequent and cursory, and nothing is done to prevent deterioration in credit risk. That is exactly what happened to the portfolios of the Cape Ann Bank, Bay State Merchants National Bank of Lawrence, and the Patriot real estate.

No Room in the Budget

Loan Operations produced statistical reports detailing the loan portfolio and its performance, including all of the past-due loans for each of the lending departments. The past-due report was circulated to all lending and credit administration areas of the bank. The report indicated an increasing incidence of past-due loans in the portfolios of the former North Shore banks (Cape Ann and Lawrence). I contacted the senior vice president, who had the responsibility for oversight of those portfolios, to point out the adverse trends apparent in those sectors. His response was that he had only one man left in the Gloucester bank who was involved in the lending area and that he was doing his best to stay on top of it. When the length of past-due loans grew to alarming proportions, I again called his attention to the impact on the portfolio of his neglect. He said that he was aware of it but that there was no room in the budget to hire more personnel. If he felt any corporate responsibility for the soundness of portfolios not originated in the Boston bank, he did not say so. Unfortunately, this inadequacy was perpetuated by the 1988 reassignment of responsibility for the Cape Ann and Bay State Merchants portfolios to what became known as BNE, North and BNE, Essex. A routine review of this SVP's performance should have highlighted the deficiency in managing the Cape Ann and Bay State portfolios, but it was apparently overlooked or ignored, and instead, he was promoted to EVP and made Credit Policy Officer.

At the time of the Conifer merger, the Patriot Bank real estate loan portfolio was transferred into the BNE, Boston Real Estate Department, and many of the former Patriot account officers left. The Patriot portfolio then suffered the same fate as the former Cape Ann and Lawrence portfolios. Three years after the Patriot merger, the 1988 Loan Review Report of the Real Estate Department cited the fact that the $500 million Patriot portfolio was still regarded as a separate portfolio and that the lack of attention and proper management rendered it impossible to review the loans for appropriate credit ratings. The BNE officers' lack of attention ultimately resulted in a large number of preventable losses.

Abrogation of Executive Leadership

In early 1989, a meeting was called by the Credit Policy Officer for the corporation. Although all were aware that it was to discuss credit related matters, the full purpose of the meeting apparently had not been made absolutely clear to all attendees: to give Walter Connolly an idea of rough estimates for loan losses for the fourth quarter of 1988. The meeting was held in a conference room at BNE, Boston. Present were Dick Driscoll (chairman of BNE), Walter Connolly (chairman of BNE Corp.), Tom Wilson (president of BNE), David Falwell (executive vice president and Credit Policy Officer), Bob Becker (Senior Credit Officer for BNE, Essex), Ferd Kelley (Senior Credit Officer for BNE,

Worcester), Wally Marcella (Senior Credit Officer for BNE, North), Lawrence Kelley (senior vice president, Loan Review), Steve Steinour (senior vice president, Controlled Loan), and myself. Driscoll started the meeting by introducing everyone and explaining their functions to Walter and instructing the rest of us as to how we were to proceed. As we started around the table, the first to respond was Marcella, who indicated a rough dollar amount he thought should be charged off out of the loans for which BNE, North was responsible. The next in line was Bob Becker from BNE, Essex. He said he could give an estimate for losses out of their original loan portfolio, but he could not estimate what the loan losses would be in the Lawrence/Gloucester loans that had been added to their portfolio. Walter Connolly broke in, insisting that he wanted an estimate of the losses. To his credit, Bob said he refused to make an estimate of loan losses in a portfolio about which they knew practically nothing. The Lawrence and Gloucester files they received had little or no information in them; what information they had was very stale, none of the loans were rated, and a high percentage of the loans was well past due. In addition, Loan Operations in Boston had refused to send them either the original notes evidencing the debt or copies of them or other documentation, which they might have. Under the circumstances, he felt that making any guess would be meaningless and irresponsible. Connolly abruptly stood up and asked, "Who is responsible for this? Is this in your area, Credit Policy Officer?" The Credit Policy Officer assured him he would take care of it immediately. Connolly walked out of the room, and the meeting was over, along with the perfect opportunity for Connolly to have shown some real leadership. An executive-level discussion addressing the unavoidable implications of this astonishing level of neglect, the arrogant refusal of Loan Operations to provide the requested information and to cooperate with the lending group, and the policy and process changes that should have averted disaster never happened.

The CPO's solution was to create an emergency task force drawn primarily from account officers in all areas of the northeast affiliated banks and to send them up to Bank of New England, North and Bank of New England Essex. They were to review and rate all of the loans of the former Cape Ann and Lawrence banks that had been reassigned to them as well as their original portfolios. The members of the task force were to stay in motels there until the rating of all the loans had been completed. The Loan Review Department in Boston would have been the logical administrator of the task force because all of the top reviewing officers in it were former bank examiners and had extensive loan review experience, but for some reason, none of its members were either included or consulted. The task force faced the same problem to which Becker had alluded regarding the Gloucester and Lawrence portfolios (i.e., the disarray one could expect in a loan portfolio virtually abandoned for two years). The files were devoid of any current information, contact with the borrowers had been completely neglected, a very high percentage of the loans were past due on principal and interest, documentation had been lost, and the requisite insurance policies had long expired. Under the circumstances, accurate rating of the loans was all but impossible. Making matters worse, most of the members of the task force had no prior experience in rating the loans to small commercial businesses and real estate developers—the bulk of the portfolio. They projected losses ultimately approaching some $30 million, which may or may not have been excessive.

Senior management in Boston attributed the losses in the north to a decline in the real estate market in southern New Hampshire and northern Massachusetts and to poorly trained account officers and weak management in Bank of New England, North, studiously avoiding appropriate assignment of blame for the fact that the transferred portfolios had been grossly neglected and left to deteriorate by the SVP in Boston who had responsibility for their oversight. Had the lack of attentive management been addressed when the Cape Ann and Lawrence officers left, what had been portfolios of average-quality small bank loans would not have produced the debacle that followed. The incident did heighten regulator concern, however, and prompted further scrutiny into BNENA Boston's credit administration and the adequacy of the loss reserves in particular. Their further and more rigorous scrutiny disclosed serious weaknesses within the BNENA real estate and communications portfolios and led to the forced replacement of senior management and, some eighteen months later, to the bankruptcy of the Bank of New England Corporation.

Epilogue

This book is written in the hope that the lessons to be learned from the failure of Bank of New England Corp. might be more readable and more readily accepted by a chronological presentation, the issues raised and discussed at some length, and the inclusion of the of memos and letters written as the portfolio deteriorated. The names and titles of the major players intimately involved in the process are included.

Following are several quotes; the first is quoted in the introduction and is from a presentation given by M. Hoenig, president of the Federal Reserve Bank of Kansas City, in October 2006.[23]

> My purpose in reviewing these stories with you today is not that I think a return to a 1980s-style crisis is imminent. Certainly, banking conditions today are good: strong earnings, good asset quality, no bank failures in more than two years. However, those who, in the early 1980s, predicted an endless rise in energy markets and real estate values were as

> confident in their outlook as we are today. And, certainly, the same rules and lessons continue to apply in banking and finance.
>
> Although the world has changed during the last quarter of a century, at least one thing has not—human nature. As I mentioned earlier, greed, pride, arrogance and other human frailties are often at the root of bad banking decisions, and those qualities remain with us today. They still motivate behavior as they have in the past, and, in many cases, these frailties keep us from acting on the lessons we should have learned from previous generations. In addition, no matter how sophisticated we think current analytical tools, management information systems and financial instruments are the most critical element in banking is still individual experience and judgment. In the end, bank employees, and, I would stress to this audience, bank directors, are still making the important decisions. The quality of those decisions will always depend on human characteristics and our ability to learn from the past.

Greed, pride, arrogance, and other human frailties are indeed at the bottom of most banking problems. As with many other endeavors, bigger always appears to be better in a competitive environment. In banking, the rewards for senior management of large banks are not only monetary, although these are important incentives, but also include social recognition: trusteeships of local hospitals, museums, colleges, and universities and symphony orchestras as well as invitations to become corporate directors. All of these are pretty heady incentives. These factors undoubtedly entered into the motivation for growth at Bank of New England. Unfortunately, there was a lack of strong, objective leadership at the top. It led to the appointment of individuals to positions of responsibility on the basis of personal relationships rather than demonstrated capability, a process that gradually permeated all of senior management. As David Falwell once patiently explained to me, "You don't understand. The major responsibility of a senior manager is to get along with the other members of senior management." This "go along to get along" management style ultimately resulted a virtual destruction of the principle of checks and balances between credit administration procedures designed to monitor and manage credit risk on the one hand and the goals of increased market share and loan growth on the other. The resultant erosion of sound lending principles for the sake of volume ultimately resulted in the failure of the institution, and the conduct was alluded to by the FDIC in the following excerpt from Richard Driscoll's deposition in the matter of *Branch v. Federal Deposit Insurance Corporation*, vol. 1, April 19, 1995, page 23:

> Q: Was the receipt of this letter [from the FDIC to Driscoll's attorney] the first time you became aware that the FDIC was asserting claims against you for breach of fiduciary duty and mismanagement and gross negligence in connection with the failure of BNEC?

> A: Well, let me see if I can explain what my understanding was. My understanding was that a group of officers were in a legal action with the FDIC, and my representative in that was [attorney]. So I always knew that there was an action and my interests were being represented by [attorney].

The third quote is from the summary regarding the Bank of New England by Chairman Gonzalez of the US House of Representatives Committee on Banking and Urban Affairs:

> The study provides the most thorough autopsy of a major bank collapse ever undertaken by the Committee.
>
> This study of the Bank of New England collapse provides extremely valuable case history of management and regulatory failure. Bank of New England must be a lesson learned, not repeated.

Chairman Gonzalez cites the need for the Bank of New England lesson to be learned and not repeated. That was some sixteen years ago, and judging from the credit problems the banking system is currently experiencing, the lesson was either never learned beyond the few who read the report or those who experienced the consequences of the failure personally, or the "greed, pride, arrogance, and other human frailties" referred to by President Hoenig fifteen years later again took over the common sense of those banks responsible for today's subprime credit crunch. After all, the REIT crisis of the 1970s, the oil-related crisis involving Penn Square, and the real estate problems of the 1980s had many things in common, not the least of which was the willingness of banks to lend money to organizations that, in turn, would lend the money to borrowers that banks had determined were not acceptable banking risks. Other common traits include the redefining of credit risks to accommodate desires for increased volume, a blind willingness to rely on the credit judgment of others to justify loan participations, and the common philosophy that if other large banks appear to be doing it, it must be all right.

One step that would have gone a long way toward solving part of the problem of erosion of credit standards for the sake of growth would have been to require that the SVP who was in charge of the Loan Review Department of the bank report directly to the Board of Directors, a suggestion rejected at BNENA. Ideally, in order to ensure independence of thought and to avoid issues of "hierarchy" within the organization, the title and compensation should be the same as that given to the Senior Lending Officer. In addition, the head of Loan Review should have the authority to prevent innovative financing by the bank until such time as a thorough review of the inherent risks in such financing has been completed and approved. If and when bank examiners discover problems in the lending area, they should insist on the above arrangement. Such a requirement by the regulators undoubtedly would be resisted by the banking community on the basis of infringement on bank management's prerogatives, but there is nothing to prevent management itself from instituting such a policy. How much damage to the economy as a whole could have been prevented had such a policy been enforced over the past thirty years? How much more in terms of earnings and solid industry growth could have been achieved?

"New from accounting, sir. Two and two is four again."

Hopefully this book will be taken and accepted by the banking community as a whole as an illustration of management weaknesses developing over time, which, left unchecked, result in the failure of institutions. Managers should think whether they are promoting people on the basis of personal relationships rather than objectively demonstrated ability. Today's banking offers new warning signs that we again are heading down the slippery slope: reverse mortgages, the purchase by banks and investors of securities backed by the same assets that failed before, and the purchase of financial derivatives, the risk in which is not clearly understood by the buying public. The problems here are one of management in general, not of banks alone. GM, Lehman Brothers, Bear Stearns, and AIG went into bankruptcy because of poor management. After a company has been successful for a certain number of years, there's a risk of complacency in management and a feeling that they can do no wrong. Management teams today must remain objective in the assignment of responsibility to make sure that all management functions are properly executed. There is no room for ineffective evaluation in capable management. Because of mergers of banks with other types of financial institutions, the resulting organizations are far bigger and more diverse than they were thirty years ago; the failure of any one has far more ramifications for the industry and the economy than was the case in the past. We are faced today with all the conditions for a perfect storm: industry czars and, in many cases, appointed senior company executives who may not really understand their businesses and are unfamiliar with the capability of the remaining managers, the increasing influence of "special interests," and an environment that presents greater and greater risk for poor management decision making.

Appendices

Charles B. M. Douglas's Résumé

Business Experience

Thirty-four years in banking, two years in industry, and eleven years in consulting with banks and individuals regarding banking matters. Specifics follow.

- 1953–1967
- Merchants National Bank/New England Merchants National Bank, Boston, Massachusetts

  Went through the officer training program and worked in various departments until assuming the position of head of the Commercial Finance Department in 1961. Was promoted to vice president in that capacity and remained there until leaving the bank to go to New York in 1967.

The Commercial Finance Department made loans secured by the assignment of accounts receivable and inventories. The loans ranged in size from $50,000 to several million, and the borrowers were engaged in a wide variety of manufacturing and wholesaling businesses. In addition, the department was given the responsibility for following and handling all of the non–real estate workout loans.

- 1967–1969

  Gray Manufacturing Company

  Was assistant to president and chairman of the board.

  Responsible for monitoring and improving performance of manufacturing plants in Michigan and New Jersey, and responsible for negotiation of union contracts.

- 1969–1980

  Irving Trust Company, New York, New York

  Joined the Irving Trust Company as a vice president in the Wall Street District II office, handling investment banking and brokerage firms, primarily making leveraged buyout loans to companies brought to us for temporary financing by investment bankers and brokers.

- 1971–1974

  Irving Trust 245 Park Avenue Office

  Became vice president and manager.

  Manager of the largest Irving Trust Company branch located at 245 Park Avenue in 1971. The office had the responsibility for lending to Fortune 500 companies headquartered in midtown Manhattan as well as providing personal banking services to employees of companies located in that area. Combined loan outstanding aggregated roughly $800 million.

- 1975–1977

- Corporate Lending Group

  Was vice president.

  The corporate lending group was formed in 1975 to handle the bank's thirty largest relationships. These consisted primarily of corporations headquartered in New York City and southern Connecticut. I had the responsibility for all of the airlines, transportation companies, and conglomerates such as ITT and GTE.

- 1977–1980

- Industry Development Department

  Became vice president and manager.

  The Industry Development Department was formed when the bank restructured its commercial lending activities into dollar denominated industrial and commercial segments rather than geographical location. The exception was the Industry Development Department, which was formed to continue to service all of the airlines, transportation companies, and conglomerates regardless of geographical location.

- 1980–1989

  New England Merchants National Bank/Bank of New England

- 1980–1981

  Controlled Loan Department

  Was vice president and manager.

  I rejoined the New England Merchants National Bank (later known as Bank of New England) in January 1980 as the vice president in charge of the department handling all of the bank's workout loans. The loans ranged in size from loans as small as $25,000 to loans of several million dollars and covered a broad spectrum of business activity.

- 1981–1989

- Loan Control

  Was senior vice president.

  Manager of the Loan Control function of the bank, which involved responsibility for the

Loan Review Department, the Controlled Loan Department, and participation as representative of credit administration, first on the Senior Loan Approval Committee and later on all loan approval committees when divisional loan approval committees were formed to consider loans between $1,000,000 and $2,000,000. All loans in excess of $2,000,000 continued to be presented to the Senior Loan Approval Committee.

Testified and deposed several times in connection with legal action resulting from collection efforts while an officer of Bank of New England and its predecessors.

- 1989–2002

  Charles Douglas & Associates, Inc.

  In June 1989, I left Bank of New England to form my own consulting company to assist banks in all areas of credit administration. In this capacity, I was called upon by banks to assist in developing workout strategies for specific loans, to establish credit policies, to develop loan review procedures and credit rating systems, to evaluate existing procedures, and to perform evaluations of bank management, both as mandated by the FDIC and by bank boards seeking an independent evaluation of lending staff capability. The largest of these assignments was to develop and implement loan review and risk rating systems for Swiss Bank Corporation in New York. The systems were adopted by the bank on a worldwide basis.

In addition, I have been called upon and deposed as an expert witness in some cases, including litigation against directors of banks closed by the regulators as well as in a suit against an accounting firm by State Street Bank. I have acted as a fact witness in other cases involving the *Trustee of Bank of New England Corp. v. the FDIC et al.*, and most recently in a case involving the *Bankruptcy Trustee for Bank of New England v. Ernst & Whinney*, the accountants for Bank of New England. I have also testified on behalf of borrowers whose loans were called when collateral values dropped below levels acceptable to the banks involved.

- 1993–2002

  Merchants Funding Corp.

  Was president and managing director.

  An associate of mine and I formed Merchants Funding Corp. in June 1993 to represent Allied Capital Corporation in the New England states. Allied is a Washington, DC,–based nonbank lender approved by the SBA and is engaged in making SBA guaranteed loans to small business as well as larger loans through their commercial real estate investment trust. We acted as a source of loans and performed the preliminary underwriting.

Education

Bowdoin College, BA, 1950

Babson College, MBA, 1965

Various seminars and courses on banking and finance matters

Other

- Scheduled speaker in training program at Bank of New England
- Conducted and participated in various seminars sponsored by Massachusetts Bankers Association
- Scheduled speaker at Arthur D. Little Management Education Institute from 1991 to 1997
- Participant as outside director in the management game graduate course at New York University

Dramatis Personae

First Appearance	Name	Title(s), Etc.
34	Chapman, Richard P.	Had recently been named President and Chairman when the author joined Merchants National Bank in 1953. Chapman had worked for Merchants, primarily in the Trust Department, since his graduation from Harvard Business School in the mid 1920s. Chairman of the Board and President of the bank in the mid to late 1960s.
87	Connolly, Walter	Chairman of Bank of New England Corporation
Author	Douglas, Charles B. M.	Office Head of Irving Trust Company's 245 Park Avenue office in New York; Senior Vice President BNENA; Officer in Charge, Loan Control; for full details, see author's resume in the Appendices.

24	Driscoll, Richard D.	Executive Vice President and Credit Policy Officer from the late 1970s to 1985. He became Chairman of the Senior Loan Approval Committee (SLAC) in 1981 and retained that position after being promoted to President of BNENA in 1985. Promoted to Chairman of Bank of New England, NA in 1987.
25	Falwell, David G.	Lending group leader; was promoted to Executive Vice President and Credit Policy Officer in 1987, when Hugh Taylor was made EVP in charge of Commercial Banking, and remained CPO through 1989. Assumed CPO for BNEC in 1988.
30	Henry B. Gonzalez	Chairman of the US House of Representatives' Committee on Banking, Finance and Urban Affairs in 1991 and the author of a staff report on the failure of the Bank of New England.
No mention	Hickey, Ed	In charge of public relations at Merchants National Bank in the mid 1950s. In his ad campaigns, he capitalized on the authority given the lending officers, featuring the "Where the man you talk to is the bank" line that ran successfully for many years. At one point, the bank's ads even claimed, "It takes two to say, 'No'".

97	Kelley, Lawrence R.	Was an ex-bank examiner hired to replace the head of the Loan Review Department when the latter retired in 1985. He was interviewed extensively by the FDIC during bankruptcy proceedings.
138	Kimball, Charles C.	Was VP and the bank's senior lender during the 1950s.
24	McAlear, Robert T.	SVP in charge of Boston Community Banking; succeeded Richard Driscoll as Credit Policy Officer for a short period in 1985, only to become the officer in charge of the Commercial Finance Department when the head of that department left the bank. Later cited (in a March 29, 1985 memo) as both Senior Vice President of BNE and Credit Policy Officer at BNE. In 1986, was made President of BNE South.
94	McCormick, Peter	President, BNENA, 1980-1985.
128	Sweeney, James	Senior Vice President of the Real Estate Department in 1984. Favored by Richard Driscoll as head of real estate lending; therefore, recommendations to look outside for really competent group leaders were ignored.
25	Taylor, Hugh M.	Senior Vice President in charge of Commercial Banking. Replaced Robert McAlear as Credit Policy Officer and was made EVP in 1985. In 1987, Taylor replaced Thomas Wilson as head of Commercial Banking.

25	Wilson, M. Thomas	Formerly EVP in charge of Commercial Banking Division but did not have the Commercial Finance Division. Wilson was made President of BNENA in 1987 when Richard Driscoll was promoted to Chairman of BNENA; at this time, Wilson also assumed the Chairmanship of the Senior Loan Approval Committee.

Acronyms

First Appearance	Acronym	Meaning
15	BNEC	Bank of New England Corporation
21	BNENA	Bank of New England, National Association (A subsidiary of BNEC)
120	CAB	US Civil Aeronautics Board
125	CATV	Cable TV (community area television)
34	CBT	Connecticut Bank & Trust Company (A subsidiary of BNEC)
39	CFD	Commercial Finance Department
162	CLM	Commercial Loan Manual
100	CSO	Customer Service Office
144	CPO	Credit Policy Officer
139	DILLIGAS	Slang expression, "Do I look like I give a shit?"

119	FCC, ICC	Federal Communications Commission, Interstate Commerce Commission
13	FDIC	Federal Deposit Insurance Corporation
26	FIFO, LIFO	Inventory systems: first in, first out, and last in, first out
164	FY, FYE	Fiscal year, fiscal year ending
59	LAC	Loan Approval Committee
153	LAOC	Loans approved out of committee
78	LDC	Less-developed countries
233	NEMNB	New England Merchants National Bank
132	NOI	Net operating income
29	OCC	Office of the Comptroller of the Currency
95	OIC	Officer in Charge
146	REIT	Real estate investment trust
164	SD/CF TD/CF CF/DS	Senior debt to cash flow Total debt to cash flow Cash flow to debt service
24	SLAC	Senior Loan Approval Committee
39	UCC	Uniform Commercial Code

The following acronyms are assumed to be understood by virtually all readers and therefore are not explained here: US, NA, the standard two-letter abbreviations of various US states, CEO, EVP, SVP, MBA, FDIC, IBM, ITT, TWA, M, MM, 10-K, and LBO.

Endnotes

1. Hoenig, Thomas M. "This Time It's Different (Or Is It?)." In Remarks by Thomas M. Hoenig, President, Federal Reserve Bank of Kansas City, 1-8. Accessed February 4, 2013. http://www.kansascityfed.org/SpeechBio/HoenigPDF/Tucson10-31-06.pdf.

2. U.S. Securities and Exchange Commission, Form 10-K, (Washington, DC: 1989), http://www.sec.gov/about/forms/form10-k.pdf

3. Douglas, Charles B.M. Charles B.M. Douglas to Richard D. Driscoll, Memorandum, "Re: General Comments," January 19, 1983. p. 1.

4. Douglas, Charles B.M. Charles B.M. Douglas to Richard D. Driscoll, Memorandum, "Re: Confidential Observations," June 23, 1983. p. 1.

5. Haig J. Boyadjian, "The Scent of Failure and the Use of Risk Analysis." Robert Morris Associates, Journal of Commercial Bank Lending, (1989).

6. Douglas, Charles B.M. Charles B.M. Douglas to Richard T. McAlear, Memorandum, March 29, 1985.

7. Douglas, Charles B.M. Charles B.M. Douglas to Richard D. Driscoll, Memorandum, "Re: Confidential Observations," October 26, 1982. pp. 1-3.

8. Douglas, Charles B.M. Charles B.M. Douglas to Richard D. Driscoll, Memorandum, "Re: Confidential Observations," June 23, 1983. p. 2.

9. U.S. Securities and Exchange Commission, Form 10-K, (Washington, DC: 1989), http://www.sec.gov/about/forms/form10-k.pdf

10. Douglas, Charles B.M. Charles B.M. Douglas to David G. Falwell, Memorandum, "Re: Loan Control," October 14, 1987. pp. 1-3.

11. Kelley, Robert F. Memorandum, "Bank of New England, N.A. Communications Group Annual Portfolio Review," August 31, 1988. p. 17.

12. U.S. Securities and Exchange Commission, Form 10-K, (Washington, DC: 1989), http://www.sec.gov/about/forms/form10-k.pdf

13. Kelley, Robert F. Memorandum, "Bank of New England, N.A. Communications Group Annual Portfolio Review," August 31, 1988. p. 12.

14. Kelley, Robert F. Memorandum, "Bank of New England, N.A. Communications Group Annual Portfolio Review," August 31, 1988. p. 26.

15. Douglas, Charles B.M. Charles B.M. Douglas to David G. Falwell, Memorandum, "Re: Loan Control," October 14, 1987. p. 2.

16. Douglas, Charles B.M. Charles B.M. Douglas to Hugh M. Taylor, Memorandum, "Re: Controls," July 19, 1985.

17. Douglas, Charles B.M. Charles B.M. Douglas to Hugh M. Taylor, Memorandum, "Re: Controls," September 24, 1985.

18. Douglas, Charles B.M. Charles B.M. Douglas to M. Thomas Wilson, Memorandum, "Re: Loan Portfolio Evaluating and Reporting," August 1, 1988. pp.1-2

19. Kelley, Lawrence R. Lawrence R. Kelley to Charles B.M. Douglas, Memorandum, "Loan Review Assessment and Plan," October 20, 1986. p.1.

20. Charles Douglas and Associates, "The Workout Department Policies & Procedures Guide," (1989).

21. Douglas, Charles B.M. Charles B.M. Douglas to David G. Falwell, Memorandum, "Loan Control," October 14, 1987, p. 2.

22. Scherer, Ron. "US Debt Jolts World Markets." The Christian Science Monitor. Last modified August 17, 2007. Accessed February 5, 2013. http://www.csmonitor.com/2007/0817/p01s02-usec.html.

23. Hoenig, Thomas M. "This Time It's Different (Or Is It?)." In Remarks by Thomas M. Hoenig, President, Federal Reserve Bank of Kansas City, 1-8. Accessed February 4, 2013. http://www.kansascityfed.org/SpeechBio/HoenigPDF/Tucson10-31-06.pdf.

24. US Printing Office Superintendent of Documents, Congressional Sales Office, Washington, D.C. Memorandum, "The Bank of New England Failure and Resolution: Staff Report to the Committee on Banking, Finance, and Urban Affairs, House of Representatives 102nd Congress, 1st Session," December 1991.

CPSIA information can be obtained
at www.ICGtesting.com
Printed in the USA
FFOW02n1825230917
40289FF

9 780692 918265